THEORY OF
UNION BARGAINING GOALS

THEORY OF
UNION
BARGAINING
GOALS

Wallace N. Atherton

PRINCETON UNIVERSITY PRESS

PRINCETON, NEW JERSEY

This book was composed in Times Roman on a Photon Pacesetter

Printed in the United States of America
by Princeton University Press, Princeton, N.J.

FOR KARYL

PREFACE

This book is concerned with a single but very important facet of the behavior of labor unions: the ways in which their bargaining objectives are determined. Attempts to come at this matter with the established conceptual apparatus of formal economic theory lead not only to a narrow focus on those elements which most readily lend themselves to such an approach, but also to assumptions about union behavior which assign those elements decisive roles as determinants. Thus, in order to suit the material to the machinery at hand, the union has been conceptualized as an economic unit like the firm, with some function of wage rates and employment replacing profits as the maximand.

Many labor economists writing outside of the context of formal theory have found this picture to be significantly incomplete. Unions, they point out, bargain about numerous variables other than wage rates. Furthermore, the prospect of a long strike may be at least as compelling a deterrent to union ambition as the expectation of a reduction in employment. It is also claimed that certain economic changes—wage gains in other industries, for example—influence union wage policies through their effects on the relative militancy of the members; such lines of causation are excluded (save as exogenous "changes in taste") from models of the union based solely upon wage-employment relationships. Finally, some critics doubt the usefulness of any theory of the union which makes no allowance for certain attributes of union structure often referred to as "political." These include differences of interest among the members, the particular interest of the leadership in institutional survival and retention in office, and the role of membership opinion in helping to define a set of potentially feasible objectives, among which the leaders can make choices consonant with other pressures and predilections.

The present work began as an attempt to cope with the diversity of elements in the problem by devising an apparatus more nearly suited to the task. The tools adopted for this purpose were no more elaborate than simple notions of probability and a little introductory set theory. The conceptual devices employed in the framework were either borrowed from existing formal theory of the union or adapted from the observational generalizations of the aforementioned critics of such theory. The essential logical structure presented in Chapters V through VII was complete before most of the rest of this book was begun. The subsequent evolution of the theoretical analysis in its entirety, as it is here progressively unfolded, was to a large extent prompted by a feeling of necessity to find some way to guide the reader gently into this departure from familiar lines of approach to the subject matter. The path selected, however, is not a mere exercise in expository strategy. The intermediate models used as stepping stones are themselves suggestive and an aid to clarity of thought. Considerable effort is made to achieve such clarity and to organize the material so that novel concepts can be absorbed gradually.

We begin, in Chapter I, with a rather narrowly selective and occasionally critical review of the existing literature on the theory of the determination of union bargaining objectives. Primary emphasis is given to those elements in this literature which are to be used in succeeding chapters. (Because of the continuing popularity among economists of the hypothesis that unions can best be viewed as seeking maximization of their members' collective wage incomes, however, several paragraphs are devoted to a discussion of its implications and—in our opinion—shortcomings.) Chapter II is a brief, informal sketch of the conceptual structure of the union as we are going to treat it—the variables to which it is responsive and the behavioral assumptions which determine its responses. This chapter is designed to give the reader a glimpse of what inspires the model we are seeking to construct.

We then commence the sequential development of the analysis which occupies the remainder of the book. It starts with a theory whose format and substance are akin to those of existing theories, then alters it by adding unfamiliar elements, one by one. In Chapter III, as the first of a succession of steps, an eclectic "economic" model is built with the aid of two provisional assumptions. These are: (1) complete internal homogeneity of preferences about bargaining objectives, and (2) perfect knowledge and foresight concerning everything relevant to the attainment of these objectives. The union's members seek higher real incomes and more leisure. The extent of their aspirations is limited by the knowledge that, beyond some point, further gains would be offset by "too much" unemployment and/or "too long" a strike. The main innovation in this chapter is the inclusion of anticipated strike length as a variable which affects union preferences concerning possible goals. In Chapter IV, the first of the two provisional assumptions is dropped:

homogeneity of preferences within the union is no longer supposed; the "economic" model of Chapter III is modified into a "politico-economic" one. Allowance is made both for differences of interest between the union's members and its leaders and for diversity of goals within the membership itself. The leadership is faced successively with specific types of external and internal threats, and we analyze in each case how the need to dispel these threats will limit the set of possible objectives among which it may safely choose. Finally, several hypotheses are offered about how the choice among "safe" alternatives might be determined.

Thus far, the analysis is carried out in ordinary English aided by graphs and a few simple equations. In Chapter V, however, the theory developed in Chapter IV is restated more precisely. Basic concepts are defined in set-theoretical language; axioms are bared and discussed. This reformulation is the means whereby, in Chapter VI, we are able at last to dispense with the second of the provisional assumptions noted above—that of our union's perfect knowledge and foresight. The theory, as now formalized, is adapted to deal with a union faced with probabilities rather than certainties. In addition, the list of variables impinging on the union is no longer restricted to those particularized in earlier chapters. As before, specific variants of the theory are developed to account for union behavior in response to specific types of external threat. In the concluding Chapter VII, additional adaptations of the probabilistic theory are addressed to the effect of internal threats to the leadership's control of the organization. At the end, an Appendix provides, for ready reference, a list of all definitions and axioms used in the last three chapters.

It is a pleasure to have this opportunity to express some measure of my gratitude to R. A. Gordon for his encouragement and many kindnesses throughout the years. It is also my good fortune that my introduction to the literature of labor economics and labor history took place under the exigent but genial auspices of Charles A. Gulick, and that I had the chance to acquire from Arthur M. Ross an appreciation of the cogent generalizations which could be drawn from perceptive observations of unions in action.

My first stumbling attempts to incorporate such generalizations in a fairly rigorous formulation were encouraged and corrected by Andreas G. Papandreou. Most of the basic elements of the formal theory presented here appeared initially in a doctoral dissertation completed under his direction, and I shall always be grateful for the patiently serious consideration and moral support he gave to this exploratory venture.

For his invaluable help as critic and proponent, I am deeply indebted to Orley Ashenfelter; and special thanks are due to Irma Adelman, not only for her helpful suggestions but for her sustained and heartening concern that this approach be pursued.

I wish to acknowledge my indebtedness to the California State University, Long Beach Foundation for the welcome aid of a faculty research grant, to the C.S.U.L.B. Audio Visual Center for preparing the graphs in publishable form, and to Susan Gabbard, Connie Kinney, Marianne Oprian, Frieda Riess, Alice Rogalski, and Linda Waller for their patience in typing and/or proofreading this and preceding versions of the manuscript.

And in conclusion, a wholehearted tribute to my wife, Karyl R. Atherton, whose own intellectual background is such that she contributed in broad measure to the general philosophical perspective which led to this endeavor; who has shared all of the enthusiasms and many of the frustrations attending its pursuit; and whose critical acumen and skill in editorial collaboration have been happily exploited.

TABLE OF CONTENTS

THEORY OF
UNION BARGAINING GOALS

Chapter I

SELECTIVE REVIEW OF THE LITERATURE

Economic theory proceeds in part from assumptions about the behavior of economic units. Thus, a very large body of theory is predicated on the widely accepted supposition that firms will react to changes in their economic environments in ways consistent with the attainment of the greatest possible expected profit. Such an assumption may be viewed as describing the firm's preference ordering over alternative situations: situation A (described in terms of price, cost, and quantity sold) will be preferred by the firm to situation B (similarly described) if it yields the greater expected profit.

As economic units, labor unions seek to influence wage rates, work rules, and other conditions under which their members are employed; and they do this by threatening their members' employers with the withholding of labor services and with other economic pressures. But there has been no agreement about union preferences similar to the productive consensus about the preferences of firms. Reder pointed out two decades ago that "... by comparison with the voluminous literature on the theories of the firm and consumer, the amount of space devoted to the theory of the union is small indeed." The observation is still valid. He ascribes this paucity of literature to "the fact that the behavior of firms and consumers can be easily interpreted as 'maximizing' while that of a union cannot."[1]

Most of the theory of the union which does exist is inspired by analogies with the theories of the firm and the household. Analogies with the firm are of two kinds. One of these is typified by Berkowitz' model:[2] the union, while not a seller of labor to the employer, is viewed as a seller of services to its members. It is concerned with its dues revenues and with the costs of acquiring them. A second analogy with the firm, employed by Dunlop,[3] uses the wage income of the membership as a revenue function and proceeds as if costs were zero. Revenue then takes the place of profit as a maximand. Analogies with

[1] Melvin W. Reder, "The Theory of Union Wage Policy," *Review of Economics and Statistics,* XXXIV (Feb. 1952), p. 34.

[2] Monroe Berkowitz, "The Economics of Trade Union Organization and Administration," *Industrial and Labor Relations Review,* Vol. 7 (July 1954), p. 575.

[3] John T. Dunlop, *Wage Determination Under Trade Unions* (New York: Macmillan Co., 1944 and Augustus M. Kelley, 1950).

the household have been used by Fellner[4] and Cartter,[5] and Dunlop's model can be recast in this form. In these theories, the union is interested in both wages and employment, but these are competing goods: the union's indifference map shows its hierarchy of preferences among the conceivable outcomes. But in the ordinary case, the wage-employment combinations which it might achieve are limited to those on the employer's labor demand curve. The union's optimum lies at the point where this latter curve is tangent to one of its indifference curves.

Most of the present chapter is devoted to a discussion of this existing literature. In succeeding chapters, we extend the analysis of union objectives to incorporate two elements which have hitherto failed to appear in formal theories. One of these is the role of expected strike lengths as determinants of a union's goals. Strikes involve monetary losses both for the union's members and for its treasury. Hence, preferences among attainable wage-employment combinations may be affected substantially by anticipations about the strike lengths necessary to gain them.

The second missing element was pointed out by Mason[6] when he likened the union to a cartel. Unions are often composed of groups whose preferences diverge in some respects. Furthermore, groups which find the union's policies to be insufficiently compatible with their own goals may leave it (or try to alter its leadership, or undermine its programs) with greater or less difficulty, depending on the circumstances. Since the loss of affiiliated groups will usually harm the union, its leadership faces the task of finding a compromise sufficiently satisfactory to all or most of its members to keep the union together. This aspect of union policy making has often been discussed—perhaps most effectively by Ross[7]—but has not been treated formally. Much of this book from Chapter IV on is an attempt to incorporate it satisfactorily into the theory of the union.

Unions are not the only cartel-like organizations composed of groups whose preferences and interests are not identical and which may, if sufficiently dissatisfied, harm the organization by leaving it. Producer cartels and some cooperatives face similar problems.[8] So do

[4] William Fellner, *Competition Among the Few* (New York: Alfred A. Knopf, 1949).

[5] Allan M. Cartter, *Theory of Wages and Employment* (Homewood, Ill.: Irwin, 1959).

[6] Edward S. Mason, "Labor Monopoly and All That," *Proceedings of the Industrial Relations Research Association,* 1955, p. 188.

[7] Arthur M. Ross, *Trade Union Wage Policy* (Berkeley and Los Angeles: University of California Press, 1948 and 1956).

[8] Cf. Benjamin Higgins, *What Do Economists Know?* (Melbourne: Melbourne University Press, 1961), p. 24.

political parties and coalitions of such parties. Successful theorizing about the problems of one type of "carteloid" organization may be helpful in dealing with others. We have not, however, attempted in this work to extend our analysis to groups other than labor unions.

Before going further, it seems worthwhile to point out the limits of our inquiry. This is not a book about bargaining theory. When we consider the phenomenon of collective bargaining over wages and other matters between employers and unions, we need three kinds of theory:

1. We need a theory of the employer's "aims," which can be thought of as a preference ordering over the various outcomes which might be achieved. This involves application of the theory of the firm.

2. We also need a theory of the union's preference ordering over the same list of possible outcomes. It is this problem which is the sole concern of this book.

3. Finally, given the preferences of the bargainers, we need a theory which will predict the outcome. This is the province of bargaining theory, and does not lie within the scope of this volume.

A second limitation of this study is that it is concerned with only one part of union activity: the formulation of goals which the union will try to achieve by bargaining with and putting economic pressure on the employer. Unions also seek to advance their members' interests in other ways: for example, by securing favorable legislation. But this and certain other aspects of trade unionism lie beyond our concerns.

We turn now to a survey of some of the existing theory of the union and to the selection from it of those elements which we shall incorporate in our own analysis.

Let us start with the idea that unions are interested in the wage rates which their members receive. In theorizing about union behavior, many writers have found it useful to suppose that unions are interested *only* in wage income, and that they are concerned with a single rate rather than with a long list of rates pertaining to various occupational and other categories of labor. For the time being, we shall make use of this simplifying assumption. It will be helpful to think of a union which bargains about a single money wage rate paid per unit of time (rather than per unit of output), to suppose the work-week to be fixed in length, and to ignore the many other variables about which actual unions formulate policies and bargain.

Workers, and the unions which represent them, may be presumed to prefer more wages to less. Is there any upper limit to the wage rate a union might seek? Economic theory suggests an obvious reason for supposing that there is one. The quantity of employment available to the workers which the union represents varies inversely with the wage rate. Given the technological possibilities known and available to the firm, the prices of inputs other than labor, and the state of demand for the firm's output, higher wage rates will operate to reduce the quantity of labor demanded in two ways. First, higher wage rates mean higher costs, and these in turn imply ordinarily a reduction of the rate of output at which profit will be at a maximum. Second, higher labor costs may, depending on the available techniques, induce the firm to substitute other inputs for the labor whose price has risen. While workers and their unions prefer higher wage rates to lower ones, they may also be supposed to prefer more employment to less. Thus, the inverse relation between wages and employment may leave the union with an optimum wage rate above which it does not care to go.

To put the matter in different words, the union may be regarded as possessing a preference ordering over alternative combinations each consisting of two elements: a wage rate per unit of time and a quantity of employment. Graphically, this may be represented by an indifference map, drawn conventionally with the wage rate on the vertical axis and employment on the horizontal one. With the workweek fixed by assumption (to avoid introducing leisure as a third objective), "employment" must be interpreted as the number of workers employed. If the union is indifferent either to wages or to employment, the indifference curves will be straight lines parallel, respectively, to the vertical or the horizontal axis. If the union regards wages and employment as substitutes, the curves will be negatively sloped. It is usually further supposed that as the wage rate falls the amount of employment which would *just* compensate the union for an additional one-unit wage cut increases. That is, the curves are "convex from below"; as the wage falls so do the absolute values of their slopes.

While the indifference map shows all imaginable wage-employment combinations, the union's choice will be limited. It is usually the case that, although the wage may be collectively bargained, the employer is free to determine the quantity of labor he hires. The union's choice is then limited in the first instance to points on the employer's labor demand (marginal revenue product) curve. It cannot be sure of getting its pick of these; but it can be certain that all points to the right of the demand curve are out of bounds. Its optimum is represented by the tangency of that curve with the highest indifference curve which it touches.

In the less common event that the union bargains about the quantity of employment as well as the wage rate, the employer's average product curve represents a final barrier to even a very powerful union;[9] and this boundary, like the ordinary labor demand curve, is one along which higher wages can be gained only by acquiescing in less employment.

Fellner appears to have been the first to use the indifference map explicitly in the analysis of union behavior. He stops short of framing very specific hypotheses about the shapes of these maps. In his formulation, indifference curves portraying the union's preference ordering may be parallel to the employment (horizontal) axis (i.e. the union is indifferent about employment), or wages and employment may be substitutes. As we move away from the origin, higher indifference curves represent successively preferred situations at least up to some level. There may—but need not—be a most preferred indifference curve beyond which the union would not wish to go because, despite higher wages and/or employment, such a move would be "distinctly harmful to its public relations and its relations with management when the membership exerts no effective pressure for such a wage level."[10]

Both Dunlop and Cartter present specific hypotheses about the shapes of typical union indifference maps, and these are contradictory. The former regards as the most suitable union maximand the total wage income accruing to the membership.[11] From the employer's viewpoint, this is the part of his wage bill paid to union members. The membership whose wage income is to be maximized may consist of members in good standing under the union's rules, but might also be those workers needed to win a strike or bargaining election, or a politically potent subset of the official membership list. A wage-membership function shows the "total amount of labor that will be attached to the union at each wage rate." If we place the wage rate and membership on the vertical and horizontal axes, respectively, this function may be parallel to the vertical axis (as it would be in a "closed union") or may be positively sloped. "The concept envisages complete organization or a given degree of unionization"; it "is a reflection of the leadership's view of the willingness of individuals to become affiliated as a consequence of wage rates alone."[12]

[9] Fellner, *Competition Among the Few*, p. 258.
[10] *Ibid.*, p. 256.
[11] Dunlop, *Wage Determination Under Trade Unions*, p. 44.
[12] *Ibid.*, pp. 33, 34.

Dunlop's conclusions about the implications of wage bill maximization are the following. The wage bill maximizing union faces a negatively sloped labor demand curve. It possesses a wage-membership
function which is either vertical or positively sloped. The greatest
wage bill on the labor demand curve is (by definition) found at the
point where demand is unit-elastic. The union will prefer this point to
all others, according to Dunlop, if the intersection of the wage-
membership and labor demand functions lies below (and to the right
of) it. If this intersection point lies above (and to the left of) the unit-
elastic point, then the union will prefer this intersection to all other
points. In Figure 1-1, *AB* represents the labor demand curve. *G* is the
unit-elastic point; demand for labor is elastic above *G* and inelastic
below it. *DF* and *CE* are two alternative wage-membership functions.
If the wage-membership line were *DF*, the union's optimum would lie
at *H*. If the wage-membership line were *CE*, this optimum would lie at
G. Whatever the shape of its wage-membership function, the union
will always be best off at some point on the segment *AG*.

These conclusions follow from the premise of wage bill maximization if the labor market is completely organized. (They also follow if
employment of nonunionists occurs only when all members have jobs.)
This seems to be assumed implicitly in Dunlop's presentation of his
model; the horizontal axis of a diagram similar to Figure 1-1 is used
interchangeably for "workers" and "members," and at one point he
refers to the membership function as an "employment function."[13]

However, Dunlop's stated assumption is not complete organization
but (as noted above) either "complete organization *or* a given degree
of unionization" (italics added). The latter phrase is equivocal. But
however it is construed, some of Dunlop's conclusions fail to follow
from his premise if this "degree" is less than one hundred percent.

Before taking up the possible alternatives of what is meant by "a
given degree of unionization," we will find it fruitful to observe the
significance acquired by the curves in Figure 1-1 as soon as the
assumption of complete unionization is abandoned: the employment
shown by the labor demand function to correspond to any wage rate
may include some nonmembers. And the membership shown by the
wage-membership function to correspond to any wage rate may include some unionists who are unemployed. Point *H*, where the two
functions intersect, then has almost no significance. The wage at that
point is one at which the number of employed workers (members plus

---

[13] *Ibid.*, p. 40.

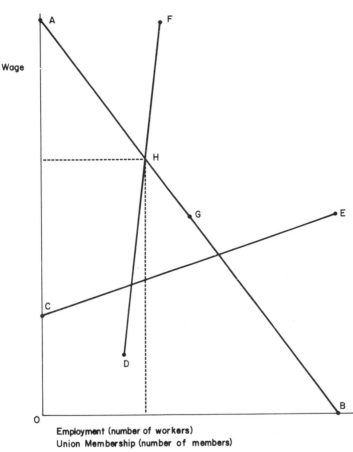

Figure 1-1

nonmembers) happens to equal the number of union members (employed plus jobless). Unless we know how many *employed members* there are at each wage rate, the location of the wage which will maximize membership wage income is unknown.

Returning now to Dunlop's "given degree of unionization," one possible interpretation of this phrase is that the ratio of members to employees is constant at all wage rates. In that event, the optimum of the wage-bill maximizing union will *always* be at the unit-elastic point (such as *G* in Figure 1-1) regardless of the location of the wage-membership function. (But this function must be so drawn as to jibe with the assumed ratio of members to employees.) For the wage which maximizes the total wage bill will also be the wage which maximizes the members' share of it.

Alternatively, "given degree of unionization" could mean constancy, at all wage rates, of the ratio of the number of union members (employed or not) to the number of workers (employed or not) attached to the labor market in question. In this case, the members' wage income may find its maximum at *any* point on the labor demand curve, even in its inelastic segment. Just where this maximum lies depends on the precise way in which the number of employed members varies with the wage rate.

To explore the implications of wage bill maximization more thoroughly, it will be useful to draw the indifference map of a union with such an aim. Dunlop did not draw such a map, but his hypothesis implies it. The curves are equilateral hyperbolae asymptotic to the axes, so that the total wage bill is constant along any one curve. Higher wage bills are always preferred to lower ones; such a union must be indifferent as to whether a given sum is split among a larger or a smaller group of members.

In Figure 1-2 are shown three union indifference curves representing wage bills of $400 (*JK*), $1000 (*LP*), and $4000 (*QR*). The market supply curve is *CS*, the wage membership function *CM*, and the labor demand curve *AD*. The intersection of demand and supply curves at *W* yields a competitive wage rate of $10; attainable total wage bills consistent with the available labor supply are found on the labor demand curve in its segment *AW*. *T* is the unit-elastic point on the demand curve where the total wage bill would be maximized. But the union is interested in the membership wage bill rather than the total. To find the members' wage bill, we must have a curve showing the number of employed members at each wage rate.

FGC is assumed to be such a members' wage-employment curve. It cannot be deduced from anything else on the graph; it depends upon whatever circumstances determine the mix of members and nonmembers among those employed at various wage rates. The only necessary restriction on it is that it may lie neither to the right of *AD* (i.e. the number of employed members cannot exceed the number of employees) nor to the right of *CM* (i.e. the number of employed members cannot exceed the number of members). The shape of the curve depends on both membership and employment; it shows the number of workers who fall into both of these categories at each wage rate. Because employment and the wage rate are inversely related,

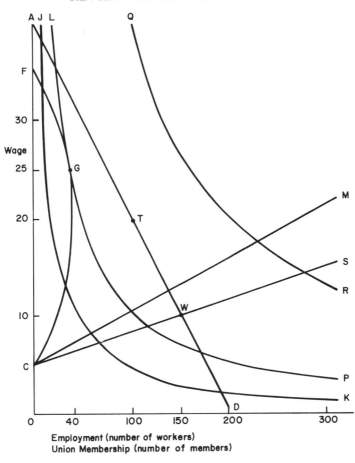

Figure 1-2

while membership and the wage rate will very likely be directly related, the slope of our curve showing employed members will almost certainly change sign at some wage. Only if there were 100% unionization would the members' wage-employment curve coincide with segment *A W* of the labor demand curve.

If one follows out the implications of maximization of the membership wage bill, it is on this new curve that the union's optimum will be found. In Figure 1-2, the optimum wage is $25, corresponding to point *G,* where *FGC* is tangent to the highest attainable membership wage bill ($1000). As the figure is drawn, this wage happens to lie in the elastic segment of the labor demand curve. (But for the members, it is the unit-elastic point.) By varying the assumed shape of segment *FGC*, we can get any optimum wage between $5 and $40. (An optimum below the competitive rate, while it seems most unlikely as a practical matter, is logically possible even though, if achieved, it would imply excess demand.)

Depending upon the shape of the members' wage-employment curve, then, a wage bill maximizing union might seek an optimum implying any point on the labor demand curve. Under conditions of incomplete unionization, Dunlop's conclusions (that such a union will never seek a wage either in the inelastic portion of the labor demand curve or below the intersection of that curve with the wage-membership function) lose their validity.

Generally, our analysis suggests that if most employees are regarded by a wage bill maximizing union as "members," the optimum will lie close to the unit-elastic point. A somewhat lower wage would be optimal for the union whose constituency is dominated by workers whose job tenures are relatively insecure. In at least two cases, a union might wish to go up the demand curve into the elastic zone. In the first of these, higher wage rates lead to a substantial influx of members. In the second, the membership of the union is dominated by workers who know they will not be affected personally by even fairly substantial layoffs. These two cases are reminiscent, respectively, of the new union which must sell the desirability of affiliation to a group of workers and of the union limited to or dominated by a minority distinguished from other employees by skill or some other attribute leading to job security.

We shall not discuss the several alternative maximands which Dunlop analyzes; he regards them as less generally appropriate than the membership wage bill but possibly relevant for some unions. These are: the sum of the private wage bill plus public payments to unemployed members, the net wage bill of employed members after deductions for intraunion transfers to unemployed unionists, the average wage income of members, the amount of employment, and—introduced but discarded as irrelevant—the collective surplus over minimum offer prices of employed members.[14] A more basic question, to which we shall soon return, is that of the grounds for supposing that unions seek maximization of the wage bill in the first place.

Cartter postulates a union wage-employment indifference map which differs from Dunlop's. Figures 1-3 and 1-4 are taken from his

[14] *Ibid.*, pp. 36–41.

Theory of Wages and Employment.[15] The shape of the curves depends upon the existing wage and employment level. At the point representing these values (*P* in both figures), the slope of the indifference curve passing through it changes suddenly, so that very large changes in either variable are necessary to compensate the union for small declines in the other. Higher and lower indifference curves have similar near-kinks. The shape of Cartter's union preference map stems from his observation that unions, when faced with increases in the demand for labor, "are most likely to have a higher order of preference for wage increases" but, when confronted with decreases in demand, "are likely to resist any wage reductions despite the inroads this policy may make on employment."[16] The point of tangency between a labor demand curve (such as *D* in Figure 1-3) and a union indifference curve shows the wage-employment combination which the union would prefer to all others if restricted to that particular demand curve. By superimposing a set of demand curves on the union's indifference map, Cartter obtains a set of such tangency points describing the union's "wage preference path."

Cartter's explicit union indifference map varies from Dunlop's implicit one in two important ways. First, the curves of the former are not characterized by a constant wage bill. The union may prefer a smaller wage bill to a larger, depending on how it is distributed. In Figure 1-3, as we move away in either direction from point *P* along the indifference curve on which it lies, a larger wage bill is required to keep the union just as happy as it was at *P*. Second, the shape of the curves depends upon the present wage-employment package. In Figure 1-4, let us start at *P* and suppose that a change in demand leads to a change in employment but no wage change. There will now be a new *P,* a new indifference map, and a new wage preference path.

Cartter's map is presented as typical but not universal. One exception, suggested by Cartter and F. Ray Marshall in a 1967 volume,[17] is that of the union with much unemployment among its constituents. Its willingness to forego aggressive wage policies until the job situation is improved is reflected by a wage preference path whose slope is near-zero through and well to the right of the current wage-employment combination, and turns sharply upward only when satisfactory employment is restored.

[15] Reproduced with permission from Cartter, *Theory of Wages and Employment* (Homewood, Ill.: Richard D. Irwin, Inc., 1959 c.), p. 91.

[16] *Ibid.,* p. 90.

[17] Allan M. Cartter and F. Ray Marshall, *Labor Economics: Wages, Empoyment, and Trade Unionism* (Homewood, Ill.: Irwin, 1967), p. 284.

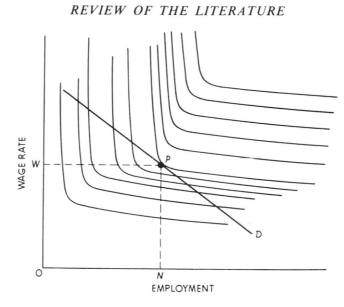

Figure 1-3

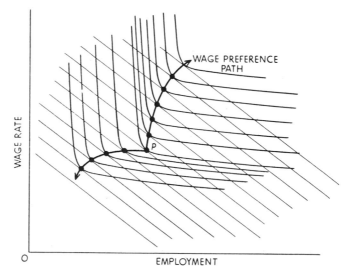

Figure 1-4

Returning to Cartter's "typical" map, the location of a near-kink (point *P*) at the existing wage-employment combination raises some difficulties. *P* is, of course, a point on the current labor demand curve. Unless demand for labor is extremely inelastic, *P* will also be the union's optimum among the points on that curve. That is, under current demand conditions, Cartter's union will want no wage higher than the one its members already receive. The inferences to be drawn from this deduction depend on what has happened since the most recent wage settlement was negotiated. If neither demand for labor nor the union's preference map has shifted, then the union must have obtained its optimum during the bargaining. (Cartter's treatment of union-employer negotiations shows, however, that he would regard this case as far from "typical.")[18] Otherwise, the ascription of optimality to the present wage-employment combination implies that the union's preference map has shifted since the last wage settlement. If the demand for labor has not also changed, then the union has come to believe that the compromise obtained was really the best available after all. If labor demand has risen since the last settlement and the employer has accordingly chosen to expand employment, then the union's preferences must have so altered that it now accepts this addition to the work force as better than the wage increase which it earlier would have preferred.

Such adjustments in union preference maps do seem reasonable up to a point. Either the acceptance of a compromise wage or an unforeseen increase in demand for labor after the conclusion of negotiations will lead to more employment than would have been forthcoming at the union's pre-settlement optimum. And once the newly hired have joined its ranks, the union will probably be responsive to their interest in retaining their jobs. But it seems unrealistic to suppose that the corresponding shift in the union preference map will normally go so far as to preclude any desire to move up the current demand curve.

A fairly small change in Cartter's model would suffice to accommodate this objection. *P* could be redefined as the union's optimum on the present labor demand curve, but not necessarily or usually the current wage-employment combination, which will often lie below and to the right of *P*. Such a redefinition would allow for unions which seek higher wage rates in the face of either constant or moderately declining demand for labor.

In contrasting Dunlop's model with his own, Cartter appears to

---

[18]Cartter, *Theory,* pp. 98–106.

make an error. It is repeated in his and Marshall's 1967 text,[19] and in a 1966 article by Galloway[20] (without, incidentally, detracting from the latter's conclusions). The error is to assume that Dunlop's wage-membership function is also his wage preference path. "If," says Cartter, "we interpret it [the membership function] as the number of workers who will wish to join the union at various wage rates, then substituting it for a supply schedule implies that the union is trying to maximize its potential membership and that membership is dependent upon the wage level obtained by the union."[21] Again, "the membership function indicates a schedule of union preferences" and "is, in fact, merely a special case of the preference path, where the relative values of wages and employment do not change markedly over the relevant portion above and below the current position."[22]

We are concerned here with the implications of wage bill maximization as Dunlop himself presented them. In the present analysis, Dunlop's version corresponds to the case of complete unionization. A preference path shows the union's optimum wage-employment combination corresponding to each labor demand curve. Along any demand curve, a Dunlopian union's optimum is found where the membership wage income is highest. This point may lie either on the membership function or to its left, as we have seen.[23] Hence, Cartter to the contrary, the wage-membership function is not always the Dunlopian union's wage preference path.

All this is illustrated in our Figure 1-5, where the indifference map of a Dunlopian union is again shown. *AF* and its parallels are labor demand curves. *ODB* connects the maximum wage bills (unit-elastic points) on these demand curves. *CDE* is the union's wage-membership function. *GHJ* and the other interrupted hyperbolae are successively higher indifference curves. To the left of line *CDE*, each hyperbola represents a constant wage bill. To the right of *CDE*, the indifference curves become horizontal lines, for the union is indifferent to employment of nonmembers. The wage preference path is *ODE*, connecting the union optima corresponding to the demand curves. Only the segment *DE* coincides with the membership function. As demand increases from the origin up to point *D*, these optima are the maximum wage bills (incomes) found at the unit-elastic points of the

[19] Cartter and Marshall, *Labor Economics*, p. 293.

[20] Lowell E. Galloway, "The Economics of the Right to Work Controversy," *Southern Economic Journal*, XXXII (January 1966), p. 311.

[21] Cartter, *Theory*, p. 86.

[22] *Ibid.*, p. 92. Also Cartter and Marshall, *Labor Economics*, p. 293.

[23] Dunlop, *Wage Determination Under Trade Unions*, p. 36.

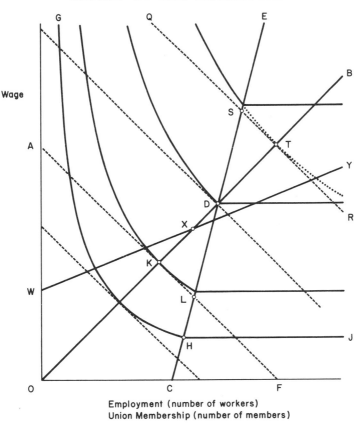

Figure 1-5

demand curves. If, for example, labor demand were *AF*, the union would prefer *K* (where the wage bill is largest) to *L* (where membership is greatest). Above *D*, the optima lie on segment *DE* of the membership function, although the possible maximum wage bills now lie to its right. (For example, on demand curve *QR*, *S* is preferred to the tangency point *T* because a movement from *S* to *T* would entail employment of nonmembers at the expense of a decline in members' incomes occasioned by the lower wage.)

In contrast to the case just discussed, the slope of the wage-membership function might be smaller than that of the line connecting the tangency points. In this case, achievement of the union's optima would imply membership in excess of employment at relatively high levels of labor demand rather than at relatively low ones. We shall illustrate this possibility with a final look at Figure 1-5. Let *WXY*, rather than *CDE*, be the wage-membership function. The preference path will now be *WXB*.

Now that the nature of Dunlop's implicit wage preference path has been clarified, we return to the conflict between Dunlop's and Cartter's hypotheses concerning the wage-employment preferences of typical unions. Unfortunately, we cannot test them by tracing actual wage preference paths from recorded wage agreements. A basic reason is that the wage rates for which unions settle are not necessarily those which they regard as best. Another reason is that, if the preference path changes with every alteration in the actual wage-employment situation, then what Cartter and Marshall call the "historical wage-employment path" will be determined in part by many wage preference paths corresponding to different wage-employment situations which have occurred during the period being studied.[24] Cartter's hypothesis is elicited from the observation that unions push hard for higher wage rates when demand rises and seek to defend existing rates when demand falls. Dunlop, on the other hand, simply asserts the appropriateness of his model; in the Preface to the second (1950) edition of *Wage Determination Under Trade Unions,* he argues for the relevance of "economic" variables to trade union wage policies and emphasizes the economic sophistication and knowledge of many union leaders.[25] But he does not tell us why a well-informed and sophisticated union leader, or any or all of his constituents, would prefer a wage rate which maximized collective wage income to other rates twenty cents lower or fifteen cents higher.

In our opinion, one basic fault of the wage bill maximization model is its failure to take account of the implications of differences of interest among members. The analysis which follows parallels closely, but only up to a point, that made by Lindblom.[26]

If we hold leisure constant, it seems safe to think of individuals as usually preferring more income to less; and, if several individuals become partners in an enterprise, we may suppose that each will wish to see high profits in the firm so that his own income will be enhanced. Most unions present a different situation; it is dangerous to presume that every member of a union will feel better off whenever the combined income of all members is increased. Typically, unions and

---

[24]Cartter and Marshall, *Labor Economics,* p. 285.

[25]Pp. iii–vi.

[26]Charles E. Lindblom, *Unions and Capitalism* (New Haven: Yale University Press, 1949), pp. 68–75.

employers bargain over the wage rate, leaving the employer free to determine how many workers he will hire. As a consequence of this employment decision, some members will receive incomes and some may get none. An increase in the wage bill resulting from a higher wage rate, the labor demand curve being given, will be made at the expense of those members who are laid off because of the higher wage. From a purely arithmetic viewpoint, the larger sum *could* be so distributed as to leave everyone better off. But union members do not typically put their paychecks into a common pot, leaving the distribution of the sum up to their officers or to a general membership meeting. Some redistribution may occur through union channels. Thus, out-of-work benefits were fairly common in the days before public unemployment compensation programs were established.[27] A more modern practice is that of forswearing some wage gains in order to secure supplemental unemployment benefits from the employer. Sometimes, unions seek a shorter workweek more as a means of altering the distributions of available employment and income than as a move in the direction of a "better" income-leisure package. But the extent of redistribution is very limited. (Collectively bargained rules governing layoff and recall—usually involving the principle of seniority—help to decide which members will bear the burden of unemployment, but not how many.)

There is an exception to this generalization, which we shall call pure work sharing. Here, the wage rate is collectively bargained, the number of man-hours to be worked is determined by the employer, and the resulting employment is distributed among the membership by the union in accord with rules which it designs. Practices rather closely approximating pure work sharing are sometimes found, as in the longshore locals of the (west coast) International Longshoremen's and Warehousemen's Union,[28] but are not common. Under such circumstances, if the union rules provided for roughly equal distribution of work opportunities, an increase in collective wage income would imply an increase in income for every member.

But in the ordinary case, if we start at a point on the labor demand curve below Dunlop's proposed optimum and move toward wage bill maximization (unit-elasticity of demand for labor), some members are gaining higher incomes while others are losing their jobs. Since this is

[27] John G. Turnbull, C. Arthur Williams, Jr., and Earl F. Cheit, *Economic and Social Security* (New York: Ronald Press, 1957), p. 216; Dunlop, *Wage Determination Under Trade Unions*, p. 37, n. 20.

[28] Charles P. Larrowe, *Shape Up and Hiring Hall* (Berkeley: University of California Press, 1955), ch. 5.

the case, why should the union stop just when the wage bill is maximized? To be sure, competition from nonunion or rival union labor may give the leadership pause; and such pressure may affect even a union which is very powerful in its own labor market where product and labor market boundaries do not coincide. Internal dissatisfaction by unemployed members may have the same effect. But there is no reason to suppose that such pressures will cause a halt *just* at the wage where the wage bill is at a maximum. To underscore this point, let us follow a suggestion of Lindblom[29] and imagine a union in which:

(a) wage policy is determined by majority vote;
(b) every member votes exclusively for his own financial interests;
(c) the labor demand curve is known; and
(d) the order in which workers will be laid off is known.

In this case, the majority would always vote for a wage goal at which just less than half the members were unemployed. Under complete unionization, the wage preference path would lie halfway-plus-one-member between the vertical axis and the wage-membership function. Such preference paths would cross labor demand curves to the right or left of their unit-elastic points but only fortuitously at that point itself. (If such a union were successful in attaining its goals it might, like Henry Simons' union "managed faithfully in the interest of the majority of its members," expire along with the firms with which it dealt upon the death or retirement of the last remaining member.)[30]

The "model" just presented may have little validity, if only because the outvoted 49% would be likely to turn to the market place to appeal the verdict of the majority and, by so doing, educate future majorities to a selfishness both more sophisticated and more humane. (Lindblom would probably disagree with this statement, as would have Simons.) But it does illustrate the point that, except in cases of pure work sharing, there is no reason to suppose that all members or even a majority will regard as optimal the wage rate at which the wage bill is maximized.

However, there is a counter-argument, favoring a tendency toward wage-bill maximization as a goal, which economists in particular may be expected to raise. This is that there will always be a monetary incentive for some members to pay others to vote for the wage at which

[29] Lindblom, *Unions and Capitalism*, pp. 70–71.
[30] Henry Simons, "Some Reflections on Syndicalism," *Journal of Political Economy*, LII (March 1944), p. 8.

total wage income (= wage bill) would be maximized. With a free market in votes, the membership would arrive at the (for them) Pareto-optimal income-maximizing wage after all.

Readers who are not familiar with such compensation schemes in other contexts may find the following example helpful. Continue to suppose the assumptions labeled (a) through (d) above, and let us further assume the labor demand curve to be $w = \$1000 - 5e$, where w is the weekly wage and e the number of workers employed. The wage-membership function, for arithmetic convenience, is $M = 150$ regardless of the wage rate. There is complete unionization. If the union's wage goal were to be determined by a self-interested majority decision without any vote-buying, then the 76 members with the most secure job tenure would opt for a weekly wage of $\$1000 - 5(76) = \$620$. Total wage income would be $(\$620)(76) = \$47,120$, and 74 members would be unemployed.

On the labor demand curve, the chosen wage of $620 lies above and to the left of the income-maximizing wage. The latter is $500,[31] at which 100 workers would be employed, generating a total wage income of $50,000. As compared with the majority's wage goal of $620, this solution would leave 24 members better off (that is, with jobs), and 76 worse off (with a lower wage). (The other 50 members would remain unemployed.) But if vote-buying were feasible the group of 24 could then induce the 76 to agree to a wage goal of $500 in the following way: if the $500 weekly wage were achieved, each of the 24 would keep only $120 (which is still better than nothing), contributing the remainder to a fund—totaling $(\$380)(24) = \$9120$ weekly—from which each of the 76 would obtain compensation of $120, bringing their incomes back up to the $620 which each could have had as wages in the absence of the compensatory scheme.[32]

Even within the context of our four assumptions, the execution of such compensatory arrangements would require that two conditions be met. One is that those who pay for their jobs end up with net incomes larger than they could have achieved in alternative employments. The other is that the cost of making and enforcing the compensation plan be smaller than the gains to be derived. If such transaction and enforcement costs are very large, they will impede

[31] Total wage income, w times e, is maximized at the unit-elastic point, and unit-elasticity can be found half-way along a linear demand curve.

[32] A similar arrangement, again leading to choice of the wage which maximizes group income, can be imagined if the membership were large enough to yield an initial majority-preferred wage below the income-maximizing rate of $500. But in this case, one group of workers would pay another group not to work.

any tendency toward self-interested wage bill maximization. Furthermore, the characteristics of most real members of real unions may diverge from our assumptions in at least one important respect. At least the broad outlines of wage policy can usually be influenced by the members, perhaps most directly by voting on the ratification of proposed agreements. The order of layoff is often well-established. But uncertainty about the demand for labor—particularly in the future—often makes it difficult to identify very precisely just what the income-maximizing wage rate would be over the period of time covered by a collective agreement.

We conclude that, even in a democratic union each of whose members is interested exclusively in his own financial gain, several factors may impede the tendency toward seeking a wage which maximizes group income. Among these are the difficulty of identifying the wage appropriate to such a goal, and the cost of enforcing the internal compensation schemes which would induce a majority to pursue it. The fact that in the real world we do not often observe junior employees contracting to write weekly checks to senior employees *may* be attributed to these factors, but is also compatible with the hypothesis that unions really do come fairly close to maximizing membership incomes without resort to internal compensation arrangements. On balance, however, the logical argument for the prevalence of wage bill maximization based on self-interest does not seem overwhelming.

Pen attacks the presumption that wage bill maximization is a typical union goal from another quarter.

> A theory of income maximization, or another "mechanical application of the maximization principle," is powerless in the face of the very real fact that unions are sometimes prepared to make great sacrifices for a wage increase of a few cents; after this success has been achieved, a further wage increase—which might perhaps have the same effect on their income—is hardly valued at all.[33]

The sacrifices to which Pen refers must be construed to include strike losses as well as reductions in employment. If unions and their members are net utility maximizers, and if their utility functions are shaped as Pen implies, then maximization of net utility would only fortuitously imply maximizing the wage bill.

The preceding discussion assumes implicity that union preferences

---

[33] J. Pen, *The Wage Rate Under Collective Bargaining* (Cambridge, Mass.: Harvard University Press, 1959), p. 58.

are based on membership preferences alone. But a union has interests of its own, among which is its income as an organization. If we assume this income to be received entirely from dues, wage bill maximization would be in the union's financial interest if dues were levied as a percentage of membership income. But such arrangements are not commonly the case; typically, dues are levied at so many dollars per month. (Bloom and Northrup compiled both financial and membership data for eighty-six national unions in 1963. Eighty-two of them charged monthly per capita dues on a flat rate basis; the remainder accounted for less than one per cent of the combined membership of 14,054,031 claimed by the eighty-six.)[34] Thus, at a given level of dues, a union's financial interests would impel it to favor high employment, so long as the marginal cost of servicing additional members did not exceed marginal dues receipts. Such considerations suggest that, from the viewpoint of the leadership, a cautious wage policy would be optimal.

However, a union may improve its financial situation by raising the level of dues. To become effective, such increases may require a favorable vote of the members or of their elected delegates. (In the United States, such referenda are required for unions under the jurisdiction of the Landrum-Griffin Act.)[35] A union's leadership might, then, wish to obtain a wage rate high enough to induce a majority of members to favor a proposed dues increase, but, again, there is no reason to presume that this wage rate would be that at which the wage bill was maximized.

We conclude, then, that, while the Cartter preference path claims compatibility with certain observed union behavior, the Dunlop hypothesis has little to recommend it except under circumstances which approximate "pure work sharing." Of course, rejection of Dunlop's particular (wage bill maximizing) model does not detract from the significance of *Wage Determination Under Trade Unions,* nor does it deny the broader assertion that unions typically act as if they took some account of the employment implications of various wage rates.

But several writers do deny this broader assertion, and would have us jettison the labor demand curve as a constraint on union wage policy. Of these, one of the most persuasive is Arthur M. Ross. He does not say that unions lack interest in the employment of their

[34] Gordon F. Bloom and Herbert R. Northrup, *Economics of Labor Relations* (fifth edition, Homewood, Ill.: Irwin, 1965), pp. 121–22.
[35] 73 Stat. 522. Sec. 10 (a) (3).

members, nor that union leaders cannot understand economic theory. Rather, he maintains that the shapes and slopes of labor demand curves are apt to shift appreciably during the life of a collective agreement, so much so that unions are ordinarily unable to take the employment effects of the wage bargain into account. "The volume of employment associated with a given wage rate is unpredictable before the fact, and the effect of a given rate upon employment is undecipherable after the fact."[36] There are, he grants, exceptional cases, "where the employment effect is sufficiently obvious and sufficiently important to some articulate group in the union. . . ." This is most likely to occur where there is a piece rate, where labor cost is a high proportion of total cost, where the industry is highly competitive, and/or where there is incomplete unionization of the industry.[37]

Investigators have found examples of unions which appeared to regard wage rates and employment as substitutes and tempered their wage policies accordingly, of unions which pursued high wage policies in the face of substantial unemployment, and of unions about which no clear judgment can be formulated. It does not lie within our purpose to review this literature; we shall state simply that there are enough cases in the first and third categories to persuade us to consider employment as a possibly significant determinant of union preference orderings over alternative wage rates. The wage-employment indifference map will serve as a building block in further work.

However, there is much more to Ross's *Trade Union Wage Policy* than his rejection of the wage-employment relationship. His work (and especially Chapter 2) contains a number of propositions about trade union preferences. Recognition that these might be useful to the theorist (or to the econometrician) has come slowly. As early as 1950, Schultz and Myers found it fruitful to combine some of Ross's ideas with more traditional approaches.[38] Pen found Ross's work to provide "a more realistic basis for the [union's] ophelimity function" than

---

[36] Ross, *Trade Union Wage Policy,* p. 80. In appraising this statement, the reader should consider the fact that *Trade Union Wage Policy* was first published in 1948. During the preceding two decades, the U.S. economy had experienced massive shifts in demand for labor owing to the depression beginning in 1929, the recession of 1937–1938, and the beginning and ending of World War II. And in the three years immediately preceding 1948, union and employer representatives had negotiated in an atmosphere of substantial uncertainty, in which many predicted that the ongoing postwar boom would be followed soon by a severe depression. On the latter point, see R. A. Gordon, *Business Fluctuations* (second edition, New York: Harper and Row, 1961), p. 464.

[37] Arthur M. Ross, "The Tie Between Wages and Employment," *Industrial and Labor Relations Review,* Vol. 4 (Oct. 1950), pp. 99–101.

[38] George P. Shultz and Charles A. Myers, "Union Wage Decisions and Employment," *American Economic Review,* XL (June 1950), pp. 362–380.

Dunlop's.[39] In the 1960's, economists engaged in empirical investigations of labor market phenomena (such as Eckstein and Wilson)[40] found writings of Ross to be helpful in the formulation of hypotheses for statistical testing. More recently, Ashenfelter and Johnson have used some of Ross's propositions to formulate a partial model of union behavior as a stepping stone to a determinate theory of the outcome of union-employer bargaining. The latter theory leads in turn to the formulation and testing of a model explaining variations in the frequency of strikes.[41]

We shall discuss the last-mentioned model later. At this point, our immediate objective is to note some of Ross's ideas which might be incorporated in formal theories of union behavior. Consequently, the summary which follows is a selective one. Ross sees typical union members as concerned both with their real income levels and with the ratio of their own incomes to those of other groups of workers.

> The rank and file always want more. There are two circumstances under which the pressure is likely to be imperative. One is a strain upon established standards of living brought about by an inflation in the price level or by a reduction in take-home pay. When these occur simultaneously, as they did in 1945–46, the pressure is particularly great. The other is an invidious comparison with the wages, or wage increases, of other groups of workers. This comparison originates more often over the clothesline than over the lunch box.[42]

This suggests a model of worker preferences in which the utility derived from a particular wage rate becomes lower as prices rise, as hours of employment fall, as taxes increase, and as other workers' money wage rates go up. If fear of unemployment does not act as a deterrent to upward wage pressure, unwillingness to strike may play the same role, and "the union leader must take into consideration . . . the degree of inclination to strike," which depends in turn upon "the mores of the workers' community, the financial resources of the rank and file, the probable duration of the strike, the condition of the weather, and the length of time since the last strike."[43]

[39] Pen, *The Wage Rate Under Collective Bargaining,* p. 59.

[40] Otto Eckstein and Thomas A. Wilson, "The Determination of Money Wages in American Industry," *Quarterly Journal of Economics,* LXXVI (August 1962), pp. 379–414.

[41] Orley Ashenfelter and George E. Johnson, "Bargaining Theory, Trade Unions, and Industrial Strike Activity," *American Economic Review,* LIX (March 1969), pp. 35–49.

[42] Ross, *Trade Union Wage Policy,* p. 38.

[43] *Ibid.,* p. 40.

In Ross's view, organizational survival is "the central aim of the leadership."[44] Elected officials are also concerned with their own reelection and advancement.[45] The union must bargain about a wage structure, not a single rate; and members' preferences about the structure are not identical.[46] The organization will seek to resolve these differences in a way compatible with its own survival. In addition, the union may have demands of its own (such as recognition, the union shop, the checkoff) which are directly related to its survival needs rather than to membership preferences.

This view of the union suggests, to begin with, that the leaders will prefer bargaining outcomes which promise both survival of the union and their own retention in office. If there is some uncertainty about the survival implications of different possible bargaining outcomes, then the theorist may consider as possible union maximands the probability of union survival and/or the probability of reelection of the leadership.

Also, union preferences will be related in some way to those of groups within the membership. Attempts to express this relation as some sort of weighted average (where weights are based on numbers of members) are unsatisfactory.[47] The degree of threat to a union's survival in the potential disaffection of any constituent group does not necessarily depend only upon the size of that group. A group might be expected to become an object of special leadership solicitude if it were within the claimed jurisdiction of a rival union, if its adherence to the union cause were particularly crucial during strikes because the work of its members was necessary to the production process and the employer would find them difficult to replace, or if its members were but recently organized and likely to relapse into nonunion status if their wishes were not closely followed.

While Ross considers rank and file pressures to be major determinants of union wage policy, he also states that the leadership, possessing superior skill in interpreting them, will have a more or less wide range of choice among alternative policies.[48] Within this range (i.e. of bargaining outcomes promising high probabilities of both union and leadership survival), its choice may be affected by such things as pressures from employers, from the government, or other sources.

It is interesting to note that, in discussing wage structures as

[44] *Ibid.*, p. 16.
[45] *Ibid.*, p. 30.
[46] *Ibid.*, p. 31.
[47] Cf. Fellner, *Competition Among the Few*, p. 276; Cartter, *Theory*, pp. 85–86.
[48] Ross, *Trade Union Wage Policy*, p. 41.

contrasted with the general level of wages within a firm, Fellner also emphasized internal pressures.

> Existing wage structures are largely determined by the influence of various groups of workers within a given union, which depends partly upon their ability to seek alternative forms of organization in the event of discontent. Wage structures also depend on the relative influence of different unions (craft unions) which depends partly on how much harm they can do to management and to the other workers by not cooperating, that is, on what alternatives are available to management and to the other workers if they should not cooperate.[49]

In developing their above-mentioned theory of the outcome (in terms of strike length and wage increase) of union-employer negotiations, Ashenfelter and Johnson adopt some of Ross's assumptions about union goals. They see the objectives of the leadership as: "(1) the survival and growth of the union as an institution, and (2) the personal political survival of the leaders."[50] For the rank and file, the minimum negotiated wage increase which would be acceptable, y_A, depends on how long they have been out on strike. Some increase, y_0, represents the minimum acceptable to the members without a strike; once a strike begins, y_A falls as the strike lengthens. For the sake of institutional and political survival, the leadership needs a wage increase which the rank and file find acceptable. If the employer is willing to grant y_0, a contract is signed. If not, a strike ensues. It continues until y_A has fallen to a level which the firm will grant. (The firm's evaluation of the impact of alternative courses of action on its future profit stream decides whether y_0 is granted and, if it is not, the length of the resulting strike.)

Ashenfelter's and Johnson's bargaining theory generates a list of variables positively or negatively related to the probability that a strike will occur. In developing an estimating equation for use with available data, they are further involved with the theory of the union as they seek measurable determinants of y_0 (the pre-strike minimum increase acceptable to the rank and file). They expect y_0 to be high (i.e. a strike more likely) when the rate of increase of real wages has been low, when current unemployment is low, and when the employer's profits are high. The latter two determinants each affect y_0 both by raising the members' expectations and willingness to strike and by

[49] Fellner, *Competition Among the Few*, p. 261.
[50] Ashenfelter and Johnson, "Bargaining Theory . . . ," p. 36.

reducing the leaders' incentives to try to convince their constituents to take a more pessimistic view.

Thus, Ashenfelter and Johnson use a model of the union in which leaders' and members' goals diverge, in which the leadership is survival-oriented, and in which the militancy of the rank and file (insofar as this is evinced by y_0) depends on the rate of change of their real incomes, the size of the firm's profits, and the current unemployment rate. This model proves to be compatible with a determinate bargaining theory and with statistically significant coefficients relating strike activity positively to the rate of change of real wages and negatively to the unemployment rate. (The absence of a significant relationship between strike activity and profits also accords with their model, since a high profit level in relation to the wage bill operates through the firm to reduce, and through the union to enhance, the probability of a strike.)

Berkowitz looks at the union as an organization which faces the problem of allocating scarce resources—primarily its staff—among alternative uses: organizing additional locals and ministering in varying degrees to the wants of those already affiliated. The union is viewed ". . . as a seller, not of labor power, but of memberships in the organization. In this process, the union receives revenues, largely in the form of dues payments, and incurs the costs of organization and administration."[51] Not only is the avoidance of losses a condition for survival, but net revenues obtained from existing locals are normally the main source of funds for future organizing activities.

The costs of servicing existing locals include a fixed element arising primarily from initial organization. Variable costs of providing services to the membership increase with the quantity of services made available. Dues receipts depend upon membership, which in its turn also varies directly with the amount of services. Presumably, higher levels of services will imply diminishing marginal dues receipts. Since both total costs and total receipts vary with the quantity of services provided, the wise union will so act as to equate marginal costs and revenues in every local, provided that net revenues are positive. The cost of a unit of services being everywhere the same, this rule will equate marginal revenues in all locals. The solution is offered subject to two constraints. First, under existing law, a union obtains or retains the right to federal protection of its role as bargaining agent only if it commands the support of the majority of a local's potential members. (We are assuming here that the local wishes to represent

[51] Berkowitz, "The Economics of Trade Union Organization . . . ," p. 575.

those workers who are in the N.L.R.B.'s election unit, and that all union members and only union members will vote for the union. Thus, equating marginal revenues and costs will be compatible with survival of the local only if the membership at this point exceeds 50% of the eligible voters. The second constraint has to do with interdependence among the local's receipts curves. To illustrate, suppose W, X, Y, and Z to be employers competing in the product market and that, so far, only the employees of W, X, and Y have been organized. It may pay to organize a local of employees of Z and to run this local at a loss because such organization will make it possible to provide more services (one may think of higher wages) more cheaply to locals of employees of W, X, and Y. The union's net revenue from the four locals combined may thereby be increased. Finally, Berkowitz points out that internal political rivalry may deflect a union's leadership from maximization of net revenues to maximization of votes. Thus, locals may be continued at a loss because of their fealty to incumbent national officers.

In the chapters to come, there will be some applications of Berkowitz' concept of net revenue maximization, and considerable recourse—following Fellner and Cartter—to indifference maps as an expository device. But the source upon which we have drawn most heavily is the work of Arthur M. Ross. The following are among the propositions relevant to trade union preference maps which are suggested by Ross's description and analysis:

1. Usually (but not always) unions do not regard employment as a function of the wage rate. This is due, not to lack of concern or to ignorance, but to uncertainty. Hence, anticipation of unemployment does not ordinarily constitute a barrier to union wage pressure.

2. However, the prospect of a strike does often exert a restraining influence on wage demands.

3. The satisfaction which workers derive from a wage rate depends upon the real income which that wage rate implies and upon the wage rates of other groups of workers. A group of workers which has become worse off either absolutely or relatively to other workers will become less satisfied. We may infer that the group will then be more willing to strike for a given wage increase than it would have been if its situation had not deteriorated.

4. The preferences of union memers with respect to bargaining objectives are not identical.

5. Unions seek to maximize, first, the probability of union survival and, second, the probability of continuation in office of the incum-

bents. They will resolve divergent preferences of members in ways that appear most compatible with these objectives. Groups of members which are in a good position to damage the leadership will receive more attention than others.

We have already rejected the option of adopting the first of these propositions as a general rule, but unions which fit it will be compatible as special cases with some theories developed in the succeeding chapters. The other four propositions will be incorporated in these theories, but not all at once. Specifically, the second and third are treated in Chapter III, while even preliminary consideration of the fourth and fifth awaits Chapter IV.

Chapter II

THE UNION CONSTRUCT

In Chapters III through VII, we shall develop in a fairly rigorous fashion a group of closely related theories about the determination of union goals. Simplifying assumptions adopted as we begin this task are successively abandoned as we move toward more fully elaborated theories. The pace is slow, the language labored, the continuity obscured by unavoidable discussions of basic concepts and by the inclusion of graphic and arithmetic illustrative devices. There is, then, a danger that the reader, in following these apparent bypaths, may become disoriented. If he is not to lose his sense of direction while pursuing the details of our formal analysis, it is important that he carry with him a clear image of the main outlines of the structure toward which that analysis is leading. Such a picture may also prove of some use to the casual reader who will be content with a hasty glimpse of our approach.

Before beginning, therefore, we seek in this short chapter to delineate the essential characteristics of the conceptualized archetypal union with which we are concerned—the variables to which it is responsive and the way it responds to them. Our construct is, of course, itself an abstraction. It excludes many aspects of real union behavior and incorporates others in simplified form. It is here described in nontechnical language which is necessarily imprecise. Any troublesome ambiguities will, we hope, be resolved in the chapters to follow. Our concern at this juncture is merely to provide the reader with a clear enough picture of our destination to give meaning to the paths employed to reach it.

1. Our archetypal union seeks to affect the wage rates and other conditions under which its constituents are employed. It does this by bargaining with their employer(s). Essential to the bargaining process are the twin possibilities that the union will strike and thus reduce the income of the employer; and that the employer will take a strike, thus reducing the incomes of both the strikers and their union. The outcome of the bargaining process is an agreement, or "contract," stipulating what the conditions of employment shall be. The agreement is to be thought of as covering only a relatively small sector of the economy.

2. The economic well-being, or "utility," enjoyed by each of our

union's members depends on a number of variables.[1] These include the wage which the worker receives, the length of the workweek, the extent of involuntary unemployment which he experiences, the prices of goods he buys, commuting time, the temperature and noise level at the place of work, and a host of others. Some of these variables will be affected directly by the outcome of union-management negotiations; indeed they are what most of the resulting contract will be about. We refer to these as "bargainable variables." But others which affect the member's economic well-being are not matters for negotiation; these variables we call "nonbargainable." Some of the latter will not be influenced at all (or only very distantly) by the outcome of the bargaining (e.g. commuting time; the general price level.)[2] Yet other nonbargainable variables will be dependent in part on variables which *are* subject to negotiation. Employment, for example, is usually not a matter for direct negotiation in the United States; the employer ordinarily retains the right to decide *how many* workers to employ at a given time, and this number may be changed many times during the life of a contract.[3] But the level of employment in a firm may be affected by the wage provisions of the contract, and in this event we have a nonbargainable variable (employment) depending partly on a bargainable one (wage rate).

3. There is one utility-affecting variable which merits special attention. This is the length of strike, if any, which may be involved in the bargaining leading up to an agreement. The level of utility enjoyed by a member after the agreement is signed will be reduced if he has

---

[1] At the bargaining table a union represents, in effect, not only its members but, of course, their nonmember fellow workers as well. In the analysis developed in ensuing chapters we distinguish between the *members* of our archetypal union and its "constituents," reserving the latter term to refer to all persons whose conditions of employment are covered in the union-employer agreement. In the present chapter this distinction is blurred, partly in the interest of pursuing points to which its relevance is not critical, partly for the sake of readability.

[2] Many readers will object that, because the wage pressures of many unions taken together may contribute to inflation, the general price level should be treated as depending on wage rates and other bargainable variables. We accept their premise, but the conclusion does not follow. Our archetype is one of many unions in the economy, dealing with one or several employers who produce one or a few goods. The general price level is an average of thousands of prices, and our union can predict the effects of its own policies on only a very few of them. This implies a relative decentralization of bargaining which corresponds to the current situation in the United States, where wage goals are set and negotiations carried out variously by national unions, local unions, and intermediate bodies but not by the A.F.L.-C.I.O. The question is discussed more thoroughly on pages 43 through 45, below.

[3] In contrast, rules governing the order in which workers shall be laid off or recalled are typically "bargainable" and are stipulated in the collective agreement.

suffered any loss of income during such a strike. In turn, the extent of these losses depends in part on the length of the strike.

4. Thus the utility (economic well-being) experienced by a member of our union after an agreement is reached depends upon the terms of that agreement, on nonbargainable variables beyond its scope, and on the length of strike required to achieve it. The entire relationship between possible values of bargainable and nonbargainable variables and strike lengths on the one hand, and the level of utility enjoyed by a member on the other, is called the member's "utility function."

5. A member's appraisal of how good or bad a job our union is doing depends on the level of utility he is enjoying. It follows from our discussion of the utility function that this appraisal depends partly on the terms of the contract and partly on other events. For example, a one-year contract with a 5% wage increase might be quite satisfactory if obtained without a strike in a period of steady work and stable prices. But the same raise might be deemed woefully inadequate if it were won after a month on the picket line and were then eroded quickly as a consequence either of short workweeks or of inflation.

6. Each member would, of course, like to enjoy as much utility as possible. But the goals and desires of the members are not all the same. They may be roughly similar—as, other things being equal, most people prefer more money to less, having a job to being unemployed, and short strikes to long ones. But workers in different occupational categories will each be concerned with the pay rates on their own jobs; relatively junior employees will be more fearful of layoffs than senior ones; debt-bound Mr. A may be sorely troubled by the prospect of lost income due to a short strike which would bother Mr. B hardly at all. Our construct takes account of these differences in interest and outlook by treating the membership as composed of "groups." Within a group, members share common bargaining objective preferences (as represented by their members' utility functions); to some appreciable extent the preferences of different groups are unlike. These intergroup differences will be more pronounced in some cases and less so in others, but from their existence it follows that even if the leaders of our conceptualized union sought only "to follow the wishes of the membership," they would face the problem of reconciling divergent goals.

7. The leadership has the job of choosing our union's bargaining objectives and of revising its choices as negotiations proceed. It must decide which management offers would be acceptable and which it would reject; whether and when to strike; whether and on what terms

to settle. It is well informed about the wishes of the various member-groups with respect to the terms of the forthcoming agreement, about how they will react in case of a strike, and how their satisfaction with the results may be heightened or lessened by changes in important nonbargainable variables. The leaders, from their knowledge of the employer's current economic situation and prospects, must size up the extent to which he will resist demands, and estimate how long a strike—if any—might be required to achieve a particular bargaining objective. And they will also try to estimate, insofar as they can, what is likely to happen to important nonbargainable variables during the expected life of the agreement.[4]

8. Given the state of their knowledge of the situation, by what criteria do the leaders of our union-construct decide which possible objectives are superior and which inferior? On what grounds do they conclude that Contract X would be worth a month on strike but Contract Y would not? In the first place, they seek to assure the survival of the union as the bargaining representative of its constituents. If there is some external threat to the union's position (such as a rival union) they seek to dispel it. Second, our leaders wish to retain their offices in the face of any internal threats.[5] Possible Contract A will be preferred to possible Contract B if the leadership believes the probability of union survival in the case of A to be greater than in the case of B. If A and B offer equal likelihood of union survival, or if both are eminently satisfactory in this respect, then the leaders will prefer that alternative which offers the greater probability of their own retention in office.[6]

9. Our leaders, then, are not just disinterested servants of the wishes of the rank and file. But their goals and those of the several groups which constitute the membership are not unrelated. Speaking very broadly, the relation between leadership and member interests may be stated as follows: the leaders will attain their ends only if the bargaining outcome, given the length of any strike which precedes it

---

[4]This is because a union may be able to do something to offset the effects even of a nonbargainable variable which is completely beyond its control. For example, a union which expects considerable inflation in the general price level may seek to protect its members' wage gains by means of a contract clause requiring periodic "cost of living" wage adjustments. Failing this, it may decide to insist that duration of the agreement be limited to a single year.

[5]Cf. our discussion of Arthur M. Ross, *Trade Union Wage Policy,* pp. 24 through 26, above.

[6]The problem of the leaders' choice among alternatives which are acceptable on both grounds is deferred to section 15, below.

and the behavior of the nonbargainable variables while the agreement is in force, affords at least some critical minimum level of utility to each of various groups which together constitute some critical portion of the membership. If we are to go further and state just what this "critical portion of the membership" may be and where the "critical minimum levels of utility" may lie, we must first specify just what kind of threat our union or its leaders confront.

10. In later chapters we treat at considerable length four types of threats with which our union's leadership might be concerned. Two of these are external dangers: (a) the loss of representational rights through an electoral process (as, in the United States, these may be lost to a rival union or to "no union" in an election supervised by the National Labor Relations Board); and (b) the loss of these rights in an organizational strike (i.e. a strike in which the union's future role as bargaining agent is at stake). The other two are internal threats: (c) loss of leadership positions to an existing opposition faction; and (d) the creation of such an opposition where none now exists. In cases (a) and (c), the critical portion of the membership which must be satisfied is a majority of potential voters. But in (b), the number needed may be quite small (e.g. a few key workers whom the employer cannot readily replace), while in (d) it may considerably exceed a mere majority.

11. Given the specific nature of the challenge to our union or its leaders, there is for each group within the membership some critical level of utility which will just induce it to give the leaders its support. The form which this "support" must take depends, again, on the nature of the threat to institutional or leadership survival. Returning to the four cases cited above, "support" in (a) consists of voting for the incumbent union against its rival, and in (c) of voting for incumbent officers rather than for their opponents. But in case (b), "supporters" may have to risk their jobs in a strike against an employer who wants to be rid of them as well as their union, while in (d) the adherence required is merely that of passive abstention from the arduous task of setting up a viable opposition faction.

Other things being equal, the critical utility level which induces support from a group will be higher, the easier it is for members to act against the incumbent union or leadership. For example, casting a secret ballot in a government-supervised representation election at the workplace is a nearly costless and riskless act. Faced with the prospect of such an election and with a well-known and well-financed rival, an incumbent union will need to come up with a contract viewed by a majority of potential voters as excellent in order to secure their adherence. By way of contrast, suppose that a large national union and its officials face no serious external or internal rivals. Any rank and file group which tries to set up an effective opposition faction will face an effort sure to cost them a great deal of money and time. The critical minimum utility required to prevent most member groups from undertaking such a task will be relatively low. The leaders will therefore need only to produce results which are not so atrocious as to spark a sustained revolt.

12. Thus, in this construct, survival considerations dictate some responsiveness on the part of the leadership to the utility functions of the groups within the constituency which it represents. Both the proportion of the membership which must be satisfied and the levels of utility-affecting bargainable variables which must be achieved will depend on the nature and severity of the threat which the leadership faces. Generally speaking, the more acute the menace the more responsive official policy will be to the wishes of at least part of the rank and file. Changes in the utility functions of significant groups of members will affect the leadership's policies when its interests would be jeopardized if it failed to respond.

13. Given these utility functions, bargaining objectives may also alter in response to changes in expectations about the strike lengths needed to secure various possible results. These strike lengths, of course, reflect the employer's willingness to resist, which is in turn determined primarily by conditions in the product and labor markets wherein he operates. Thus variations in expected strike lengths are one important route whereby changes in economic conditions affect our union's bargaining goals and actions.

For example, suppose that a union conforming to our pattern represents workers in the X-industry. Negotiations with their employers are to begin in two months and the union leadership has chosen as its goal a package which includes an average wage increase of about fifty cents an hour. Now, however, demand for product X declines, inventories of unsold X increase. X-manufacturers will now suffer smaller losses in the event of a strike than would have been the case had demand remained strong. Should a strike occur, the length of time they will hold out before granting a fifty cent (or any given) hike will rise. Many members would resent a long strike and for that reason be likely to support (say) a rival union against the incumbent one. Perceiving this, the leaders lower their sights and prepare to settle for a smaller increase.

The revision of objectives just described takes place without any change in the utility functions of the members or the motives of the leaders. The fifty-cent package became unattractive because the expected strike it would require had lengthened; this in turn was due to reduced demand for the employer's product.

14. Another way in which changes in economic conditions may influence our union's bargaining aims is through the direct effects of those changes on the levels of utility which the members enjoy, or can be expected to enjoy. A change in the general price level, for example, may produce such effects. Suppose that—again—two months before negotiations are to begin, our union's leaders have decided to pursue an average wage increase of about fifty cents per hour. They expect to win this with no strike or at most a very brief one, and they believe that the results will gratify the members sufficiently to leave both the union and its officials securely in command. But now the Consumers' Price Index begins to rise rapidly and is expected to continue climbing. The price level is a variable in the utility functions of all groups within the membership. Furthermore, their utility functions are such that, if faced with a reduction of real income below accustomed levels, they will be ready and even eager to risk a long strike if only to restore those levels. Under these circumstances, settling for fifty cents would create widespread dissatisfaction and hence a golden opportunity for an external rival union or an internal rival faction. To prevent this, the leaders will revise their plans and push for a larger increase. Here, even if the inflation leaves the employer and his willingness to take a strike totally unaffected, the rise in prices will nonetheless influence union policy through its effects on the attitudes of the members.

The bargaining objectives of our conceptualized union are in part determined, then, by external events whose effects are transmitted through changes either in expected strike lengths or in the economic well-being of the rank and file.

15. Very often union leaders face no grave threats to institutional or political security. While survival considerations do, of course, dictate avoidance of certain policies whose unpopularity might give rise to such threats, a wide choice of possible bargaining objectives remains. In this event, what subsidiary criteria guide the leaders of our archetype? Real unions have many and various goals. One union, functioning in a highly competitive and only half-unionized industry, may be almost exclusively concerned with the organization of the nonunion half, while another is lobbying vigorously for legislative and administrative decisions—tariffs, building codes, contract awards,

and so on—which will maintain or expand employment of its members. In a third and more secure union, we may find the leaders embarked on an ambitious program to provide resorts and retirement homes for their constituents and scholarships for their constituents' children, while officials of still another seem interested mainly in elegant offices, beautiful secretaries, and generous expense accounts. What all of these and many other pursuits and aspirations of unions have in common is that they cost money. Thus it is posited that in choosing among bargaining objectives, all of which promise satisfactorily high probabilities of union survival and of retention in office, the leaders of our archetypal union will seek to maximize the organization's net revenue. By net revenue is meant, essentially, the difference between the union's gross receipts (which come mainly from dues) and the costs of providing the current level of services to members.[7] (Our leaders need not explicitly think of constrained revenue-maximization as the goal. A union which, for example, settles for less with Employer *X* because a strike, even if successful, would jeopardize its financial position in a planned effort to organize Employer *Y* is acting in accord with our hypothesis.)

16. Although the foregoing will suffice to give the outlines of the construct, to lend substance to those outlines it may be helpful to provide a glimpse of the kind of exploration it permits. This may be illustrated with a preview of the implications of a goal of net revenue maximization. Here, and throughout the following discussion, we assume the survival constraints to be understood.

As the definition of net revenue suggests, inherent in the goal of its maximization are two concerns: the first, to avoid unnecessary expenditures; the second, to at least maintain the current level of income. These two fiscal concerns, acting in concert, will often cause the leadership to adopt a more moderate policy—to settle earlier in (or without) a strike, for smaller gains—than a majority of the members would have preferred. For strikes drain a union's treasury, while higher wages may reduce employment and hence the number of dues payers and total dues receipts.

Where dues payment is voluntary, these two fiscal concerns do not "act in concert." Frugality, in these circumstances, will jeopardize the source of income. The second concern predominates and dictates pursuit, despite the costs, of a bargaining outcome whose popularity will widen or at least maintain the base of revenue. Union security provi-

---

[7] For a more detailed discussion of the concept of "net revenue maximization," see pp. 72 through 73, below.

sions, however, alter the relative importance of the two fiscal concerns in leadership considerations. To the extent that such provisions offer assurance of no diminution in revenue, the incentive to conserve present resources is unopposed and the result is the above mentioned policy-moderating effect. The more nearly a union shop with compulsory checkoff of dues is approximated, the stronger this effect will be.

Finally, whatever the union security provisions may be (and however intrinsically strong the policy-moderating effect) the extent to which a union's leaders will be able to pursue goals which deviate from their constituents' wishes will be limited if the union's laws require that proposed agreements must be ratified by membership vote before becoming effective.

The rough sketch of our archetypal union is now complete. Its members' desires for "more" are limited at some point by the costs of striking to get it, and at some other point by fear of unemployment.[8] While sharing roughly common aims, members hold diverging views on the details of what a good agreement would be, and they vary in their readiness to make sacrifices in order achieve gains. Leaders wish first to maintain the union, second to keep their positions within it, and third to conserve resources for the pursuit of subsidiary goals. Often, this third objective disposes them to settle for the minimum gains which will assure achievement of the other two. Our union's objectives are affected by events which occur in the product markets where the employer sells his goods, in the labor markets where the members sell their services, and in other segments of the economy as well. The impact of these events is transmitted through their effects on (a) the stance of the employer, and (b) the attitudes of members. Within the range of apparently feasible goals, the decision to pursue some in preference to others is shaped by the interplay of the leaders' aims, the members' wants, and the relative ease or difficulty with which groups of members can punish the leadership if they are dissatisfied.

There are, of course, other dimensions of union behavior which are not incorporated in this construct. We do not, for example, concern ourselves with those methods other than collective bargaining which unions employ to gain their ends. These lie beyond the purview of our theory. Within that purview, there is no treatment of bargaining weapons other than the strike. Also, for the sake of expository

---

[8] Even if labor demand curves were unknown and unknowable, there would be some imaginable wage increase which would cause the employer to cease operations.

economy there is no explicit mention of the role played by the union's record with respect to past contracts, contract administration, and management of internal affairs, in shaping the responses of the members to the variables of which we treat. Lastly, we have not dealt systematically with an important aspect of intraunion communications. To a limited but significant extent, leaders can and do affect the wishes (utility functions) of the members. This is not purely a matter of salesmanship. Union leaders have relatively ready access to information (from prior experience as well as current data) which most members would find difficult to acquire and, in some cases, to interpret. Hence, the membership utility functions treated as given in our models are often susceptible to some degree of change in a direction which accords with the leaders' wishes.

In conclusion, a word of caution. The reader who embarks upon the analytical development in the ensuing chapters with perceptions geared to bargaining theory may find himself confused by a persistent misapprehension of our intent. He is reminded that our theory is concerned with explaining not the final outcome of the bargaining process but, rather, the determination of union bargaining objectives.

Chapter III

INTERMEDIATE MODEL I:
ECONOMIC

We shall now set about the construction of an eclectic theory of union behavior which incorporates elements found in the works of Ross, Cartter, and others. To come at the matter as cleanly as possible, we shall employ the strategy of carrying out the construction by stages, provisionally adopting at the start a simplistic set of assumptions. Once our basic structure is formed, we shall proceed in later chapters to modify these assumptions so as to give attention to some of the complexities of union behavior which, in the present chapter, are ignored.

It will be useful at this initial stage to avoid the problems presented by divergences of preferences within a union, whether these differences be among the members or between members and leaders. To exclude consideration of such diversity, we shall assume identicalness of preference orderings within our model union: If any member prefers P to Q and is indifferent between Q and R, then every other member feels the same way, as does the union which represents them. It will be further supposed that our union includes everyone attached to the labor market in which it is involved; the words "members," "workers," and "constituents" become synonymous. Also postponed for strategic reasons is any consideration of uncertainty. Our union is not only well informed but prescient concerning conditions in its labor market. It foresees the employment which will be forthcoming at any wage rate and the length of strike necessary to obtain that wage.

At this stage, then, we are dealing with a concordant union certain of its present and future environments. Internal stresses will enter our analysis in Chapter IV, and uncertainty in Chapter VI. The first task is to build a theory which will lend itself to the subsequent accommodation of these and other complications.

The theory presented in this chapter contains one novel element. This is its incorporation of expected strike lengths as determinants of the union's preference ordering with respect to different wage goals which it might seek. Of course, expected strike lengths have appeared in bargaining theory from Hicks[1] to Ashenfelter and Johnson.[2] However, we are not concerned with bargaining theory but, rather, with the theory of the determination of the union's objectives. In formal statements of the latter type of theory, as exemplified by Dunlop and Cartter, strike lengths have hitherto played no part. We find it useful, however, to incorporate into our model of union preference formation the impact of expected strike lengths on the union's preference map before any serious bargaining takes place.[3]

To illustrate the idea involved here, suppose that a union's leaders are weighing the question of whether or not to push vigorously for a 15% wage increase. Dunlop's and Cartter's models suggest that the leaders' decision might be influenced by the expected effect of such a wage change upon employment. It seems reasonable to presume that the leaders would also be concerned with the length of strike which might be necessary to induce the employer to concede the 15%. Having made such an estimate, they would also consider whether the wage increase would be worth (in whatever sense of "worth" might be appropriate) the strike involved. As a result of such considerations, the leadership might decide that, say, a 10% increase would be a "better" goal than 15%. Thus, a theory which seeks to explain a union's preferences about alternative wage goals may incorporate the union's expectations about strike lengths, just as it may incorporate its expectations about employment effects. The parallel, indeed, is a close one: a union's appetite for higher wages may be limited either from fear of large layoffs or from fear of a long strike, or from both.

We shall speak of our union as possessing a utility function, U. This is meant to be no more than shorthand for an index of its preference ordering; "$U(A) > U(B)$" means that our union prefers A to B, and nothing more. This utility is a function of real disposable income per member, of the length of the workweek (or of its complement, the leisure-week), and of the number of workers (members) employed.

[1]J. R. Hicks, *The Theory of Wages* (London and New York: The Macmillan Company, 1932; New York: Peter Smith, 1948; New York: St. Martin's Press, 1964), Chapter VII.

[2]Ashenfelter and Johnson, "Bargaining Theory, Trade Unions, and Industrial Strike Activity," *American Economic Review,* LIX (March 1969), pp. 35–49.

[3]Recently, Daniel J. B. Mitchell has suggested that "in most cases" unions can function without direct perception of the wage-employment trade-off "because employer resistance provides a proxy for the costly information-gathering required to make the trade–off calculation." Mitchell's treatment of employer resistance is akin but not identical to my handling of expected strike lengths. Daniel J. B. Mitchell, "The Ross-Dunlop Debate Reopened," *Industrial Relations,* 11:1 (February, 1972), pp. 46–61.

The utility enjoyed from any income-leisure-employment combination depends upon the length of strike required to achieve it. Other things being equal, it is presumed that our union prefers larger real disposable incomes per member to smaller ones, greater leisure to less, and more employment to less. The first of these preferences implies in turn a predilection for higher money wages, lower taxes, and a lower price level. Shorter strikes are preferred to longer ones; and as the length of strike rises, the increment of any one "good" (such as the wage rate) which will just compensate the union for an additional day of striking may rise or remain constant, but will not fall.

Of the several variables which affect the utility experienced by our union's members, only two are bargainable directly. These are the money wage rate and the length of the workweek. Real income and therefore utility are also affected by the income tax rate and by the level of prices paid by workers for the goods which they consume, but these are parameters which our union's power cannot reach. Employment is not bargainable in our model; it is determined by the employer. But it may be regarded by the union as a function of the wage rate and workweek and thus be subject to union influence. The strike length attaching to each "package" is also decided by the employer. Since (in this chapter) our union knows what these values are, it can decide how long a strike its members shall endure.

Thus, two factors may limit our union's pursuit of higher pay and less work. They are the disutility of striking and the anticipation of unemployment.

Before the implications of this model are explored, comments on some of its assumptions appear worthwhile. The suppositions of internal harmony, of complete organization of the labor market in a single union, and of certainty about labor demand and strike lengths are, as noted earlier, dictated by expository considerations and will be dropped later. Similarly temporary are the limitation of the directly bargainable variables to a single wage rate and workweek, and the restriction of the list of nonbargainable variables to the price level, income tax rate, employment, and length of strike. Our stipulation of a single wage rate and workweek excludes temporarily any analysis of the consequences of changes in available overtime hours paid at premium rates; this defect will be remedied toward the close of the present chapter.

The remaining assumptions are intended to be realistic. Our unionists, like those Ross depicts, are concerned with real income. Aside from the workweek, however, the money wage is the only determinant of real income which the union can affect. Some readers will object at first to our characterization of the price level as beyond the union's power to affect. It may be argued that, although unions do not bargain directly over prices, the wage policies of many unions taken together will influence the general price level because of the effects of wage changes on costs and possibly aggregate demand. But an individual national or local union, even if it were to possess the knowledge and foresight with which the model union of this chapter has been endowed, could control only its own wage policies and foresee only the impacts on prices charged by its own employer(s). In the index of prices paid by the union's members, the weight allotted to the output of a single firm or even industry will be small, and may be disregarded. Where national organizations of trade unions and of employers reach "master bargains" which effectively guide specific bargains throughout much of the economy, the master bargainers may come to regard the general price level as in part a function of the general wage level. But such conditions obtain in only a few countries (Netherlands, Norway, Sweden)[4] and do not apply to the United States, where bargaining is comparatively very decentralized. Such national confederations as the Chamber of Commerce of the United States and the American Federation of Labor and Congress of Industrial Organizations have no role in deciding the wage policies of their members.

Alternatively, it may be argued that a union which is a national "wage leader" will foresee emulation of its own goals by other unions and be able to form a good idea of the eventual impact of its policies upon the general price level. To be sure, a wage gain achieved by union X may become the aim of union Y as well, if the product and labor market conditions facing the two are similar. But even if we extend the perfect knowledge enjoyed by our model union in its immediate milieu to include the wage-cost-price relationships in other economic sectors, the argument founders. A former "wage leader" which moderates its wage demands has no grounds for anticipating that others will follow its lead; and if the wage increases which the others may obtain lead to a higher price level, then its members will be left with lower real incomes than could have been had.

There is another situation in which the wage rate achieved in a single settlement might have a noteworthy impact upon the general level of prices paid by members of the union involved. If—as in a

[4]Angus Maddison, *Economic Growth in the West* (New York: W. W. Norton & Co., 1967), pp. 136–137.

geographically isolated, one-company town—the members constitute a significant proportion of the buyers in local markets for goods and services, then changes in their aggregate money income might, by affecting demand, affect local prices in the short run. But there seems no reason to suppose that this exception has much relevance.

We conclude, then, that the price level is in fact beyond the influence of even the larger unions as they formulate their bargaining policies. Of course, this conclusion does not conflict with the assertion that the wage policies of many unions taken together may have an inflationary effect.[5]

Our other assumptions probably require less defense. With rare exceptions, unions in the United States have been unable to force employers to bargain about levels of employment as well as the wage rate,[6] so that it is realistic to assume that the employer is free to maximize his profits within the constraint of a bargained wage by choosing the appropriate point on his labor demand curve. The preference for shorter strikes and more leisure may be less than universal. A brief strike may occasionally yield to its participants enough nonmonetary satisfactions to outweigh their financial losses. With respect to leisure, it may well be that even at given money incomes many people's optimum workweeks are positive. Finally, in equating "leisure" with "not working," we ignore the fact that some kinds of leisure (such as commuting) may be viewed as "nonmarket work," or even as inferior both to working and to engaging in other sorts of leisure. While a wage increase may contribute to an increase in utility partly by inducing the worker to reduce his nonmarket work time,[7] our analysis will not deal explicitly with this effect.

Using these assumptions, we may proceed to build up our analytical framework. As we do so, in this chapter and the next, the following glossary of symbols will be helpful.

I. Variables which affect utility and are bargainable:
   w is the money wage rate, in dollars per hour.
   h is the number of hours in the workweek.
   j is the number of leisure hours in the week; $j = 168 - h$.

---

[5] Price and wage control policies of the type pursued in the U.S. between August 1971 and August 1972 (as this footnote is written) do not vitiate the conclusion. Wage bargaining remains decentralized, and each bargainer must still regard the general price level as beyond its influence. Such control policies may nonetheless affect the bargainers' objectives; e.g. a union may be deterred from seeking a wage increase of a particular size because the costs of getting it approved by the authorities may appear prohibitive or, as a practical matter, infinite.

[6] Neil W. Chamberlain, *The Labor Sector* (New York: McGraw-Hill, 1956), p. 575.

[7] Richard Perlman, *Labor Theory* (New York: Wiley, 1969), pp. 14–18.

II. Variables which affect utility and are not bargainable:

t is the amount withheld for taxes from each worker's pay, in dollars per hour.

p is an index of the level of prices paid by the union's members.

e is the number of members (workers) employed (for h hours per week each).

S stands for strike length, in days.

III. Identity:

y is the weekly real disposable income per employed worker;

$$y = wh(1 - t)/p.$$

IV. Functional Relationships:

The Labor Demand Function:

$$e = e(w, h). \qquad \text{With } h \text{ fixed, } e = e(w).$$

The Strike Length Function:

$$S = S(w, h).$$

$S(w_i, h_j)$ tells us how long the union must strike in order to win an agreement fixing the wage at w_i and the workweek at h_j. When h is assumed to be given, we may write $S = S(w)$.

The Complete Utility Function:

$$U = U\left[\frac{wh(1 - t)}{p}, j, e, S\right] = U(y, j, e, S).$$

Since $j = 168 - h$, and S depends on h and w, we may write $U = U$ (y, e) when the strike length function is given.

It should be noted that this utility function is broad enough to encompass both wage-bill-maximizing and non-wage-bill-maximizing unions. The only constraints are those expressed verbally above: for example, that a higher wage rate must imply greater utility if nothing else changes. Also, it must be remembered that U is presented simply as an index of preference orderings. We are not arguing against the use of more restrictive concepts of utility when they are needed. Pen, for example, maintains that a cardinal utility concept is required for an adequate bargaining theory.[8] But for our problem of union preference formation only an ordinal concept is needed, and it seems wise to travel as lightly as we can.

[8]Pen, *The Wage Rate Under Collective Bargaining* (Cambridge, Mass.: Harvard University Press, 1959), pp. 49–50.

Partial Utility Functions:

$$X = X(y,h).$$

X is an index of the union's preference ordering over combinations of per-member income and leisure. It is presumed that the rank-ordering of such combinations will be the same whatever the level of employment or length of strike.

$$Z = Z(y,h,e) = Z(X,e).$$

Similarly, Z is an index of the union's preference ordering over combinations of per-member income, leisure, and employment. The rank-ordering of such combinations is the same for any given length of strike.

With price and tax levels given, our union's utility depends on four variables: wages, hours, employment, and strike length. In discussing the preference map which our assumptions suggest, graphic illustrations will be helpful; their use requires a succession of diagrams in which we hold one pair of variables steady while mapping preferences over the other two. Figure 3-1 shows a union's and its members' preferences among combinations of real income per person and leisure. As we move away from the origin, the successive indifference curves (X_0, X_1, etc.) represent progressively higher levels of satisfaction. Thus, in Figure 3-1, the union is indifferent between (60, \$140) and (40, \$80)—points A and B; both of these positions are superior to (60, \$100), shown as point C.

Our stipulation that, given the amount of either of these "goods," an increase in the other will raise utility requires that the curves be negatively sloped. In so drawing them as to appear convex when viewed from the origin, we are following the traditional assumption that, as the quantity of income falls and that of leisure rises, the maximum price which one would pay for one more unit of leisure will decline.

If we fix the workweek, as we shall later have occasion to do, levels of X can be designated in monetary units. When this is done, we must be careful to remember the ordinal nature of our utility concept. Again taking an example from Figure 3-1, if we set the workweek at 40 hours (and the leisure week at 128), the income on X_4 is twice as large as that on X_2 (\$160 and \$80 at points D and B, respectively). This means only that \$160 is more satisfying than \$80, not that it is twice as satisfying.

To bring employment into the picture, we draw a preference map

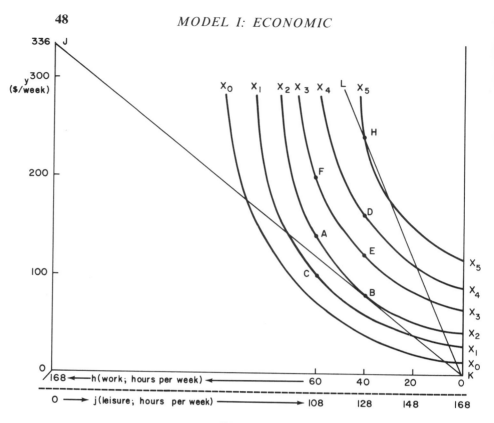

Figure 3-1

over combinations of satisfactions from the income-leisure package
(X) and the number of workers employed (e). In Figure 3-2, the
indifference curves are designated as Z_1, Z_2, etc. $Z(X,e)$ is a function
of X and e such that if (e_1,X_1) is preferred to (e_2,X_2), then $Z(e_1,X_1) >$
$Z(e_2,X_2)$; while if the union is indifferent between (e_1,X_1) and (e_2,X_2),
then $Z(e_1,X_1) = Z(e_2,X_2)$.

Each X-ordinate in Figure 3-2 stands not for a unique combination
of income and leisure, but for a set of equally satisfactory packages
thereof. And each Z-curve represents a set of equally satisfactory
combinations of income, leisure, and employment. An example may
help to fix the meaning. The curve Z_2 passes through the points ($e =$
90, $X = X_2$) and ($e = 50$, $X = X_3$). Returning to Figure 3-1, we observe that among the points on curve X_2 are ($h = 40$, $y = \$80$) and ($h$
$= 60$, $y = \$140$), while X_3 includes ($h = 40$, $y = \$120$) and ($h = 60$, $y =$
$\$200$). (These are shown as B, A, E, and F, respectively.) Therefore,

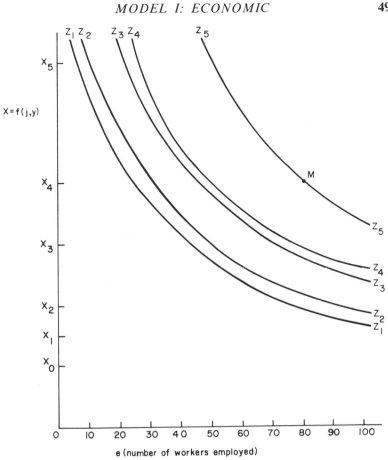

Figure 3-2

among the combinations toward which our union is indifferent are:

h	y	e
40	\$ 80	90
60	140	90
40	120	50
60	200	50

At this point, some readers may feel rebellious in view of the incongruities attendant upon the assumption of identical preference orderings. To be asked to accept, however provisionally, the supposition that, say, a low seniority worker A and high seniority worker B would both be willing to exchange A's job for a rise in B's income may appear so outrageous as to make pursuit of the argument difficult for the tenacious realist. But although we shall later discard this assumption of identicalness and devote considerable attention to the deduction of a union's preferences from those of conflicting groups within its ranks, we cannot do so at this time. For those who are resistant to working with assumptions which are not at least hypothetically plausible, it may be of some help to imagine a labor market in which, while the number of employees is decided by the employer, the choice of the individuals who will get the jobs is left up to a lottery in which everyone has an equal chance.

Returning to Figure 3-2, we observe another noteworthy peculiarity in this preference map. The vertical distances from the origin at which specific values of X are shown are, to a substantial degree, arbitrary. It is as if the axis were made of rubber. X_2 *must* be farther from the origin than X_1; so long as this condition is met the distance between them, as well as the ratios of their distances from the origin, can logically be whatever one likes. And, since we have defined no zero for X, the origin on the vertical scale is arbitrary. The employment variable, on the other hand, is measured cardinally and its axis is subject to the usual rules. Despite these peculiarities, the graph is meaningful. However one stretches or squeezes the vertical axis, the preference pattern read from the graph is the same. The numerical value of the slope of a curve at any point tells us nothing, but the signs of such values are significant.

Z, then, is an index of the satisfaction derived from various combinations of income, leisure, and employment. But this is not the last step in elaborating our union's preference pattern, for we must take into account the sacrifices, in the form of strikes, which achievement of the various levels of Z might entail. In Figure 3-3, we have one more indifference map, with Z on the vertical axis and strike lengths (S) on the other. This map tells us nothing about how long you must strike in order to obtain an income-leisure-employment package yielding, let us say, Z_5. All it shows are the union's preferences among all conceivable combinations of Z and strike length. A line such as U_4 connects all such combinations among which the union is indifferent. For example, two of the points on U_4 are ($S = 0$, $Z = Z_3$) and ($S = 10$, $Z = Z_5$). This means that our union is indifferent between:

(a) obtaining without a strike any of the income-leisure-employment combinations which appear on curve Z_3 in Figure 3-2, and

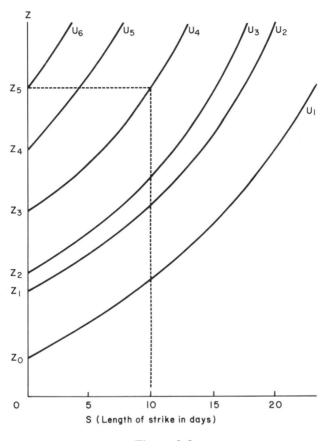

Figure 3-3

(b) obtaining after ten days on strike any of the income-leisure-employment combinations on curve Z_5.

Points to the northwest of U_4 are better; those to the southeast are worse. Z is measured on a "rubber axis" like the one used for X in Figure 3-2. The diagram is drawn to conform with our assumption that shorter strikes are preferred to longer ones.

Just as the consumer in the theory of the household is constrained by his budget to choose from a portion of his indifference map, so will our union be limited in its choice of bargaining objectives. There are two constraints to be considered. The first is the labor demand function. This function says that every value of (w,h) implies some e. Hence, given p,t and our utility function, every (w,h) implies some Z.

The second constraint is the strike length function. Under our assumption of certainty, the strike length attached to a particular goal represents the union's correct estimate of the length of time the employer(s) would hold out before granting it. For some objectives, this will be zero. At the other extreme, some goals will be unattainable. The strike length function, $S(w,h)$, says that every (w,h) implies some (zero or positive finite) S, or is unattainable.

Given $p,t, e(w,h), S(w,h)$, and the utility function, every attainable (w,h) implies some U. The union's aim, of course, is to get the highest U permitted by the two constraints.

Unfortunately, we cannot simply draw these constraints as lines on Figure 3-3 and show the union's consequent preferences among the restricted set of alternatives available to it. With respect to the strike length function, a given value of Z will not in most cases imply a *unique* strike length just sufficient to achieve it. For a particular value of Z can be had from a number of combinations of values of w, h (and j), t, p, and e which provide equal satisfactions to the union. But these combinations will not provide equal satisfactions (profits) to the employer. Hence, the S corresponding to any Z will vary, depending upon the particular values of w,h, t,p, and e.

The same is true of the labor demand function. The number of workers demanded at a particular wage rate will differ depending upon the workweek (h); with a longer workweek, fewer employees would be required to achieve the output which the firm finds it most profitable to produce.

But once we have fixed h, t, and p we *can* put our two constraints into two-dimensional diagrams—and they are diagrams of the familiar sort in which both variables are measured cardinally. Quite aside from convenience, there are good reasons for treating h, t, and p as parameters. Tax and price levels are, as we have said, beyond the reach of the bargainers' influence. The workweek is bargainable but remains standardized for long periods of time while the wage rate is involved in nearly every negotiation. So let us fix the price level at an index of 1.0, taxes at zero, the workweek at 40 hours, and the leisure-week consequently at 128. Variations in the money wage are now the only possible source of variations in the individual worker's income-leisure package. Hence, we can replace X with the wage rate and Figure 3-2, the union's X-employment preference map, with the familiar and more tractable wage-employment map shown in Figure 3-4. To each of the levels of X appearing in Figure 3-1, there now corresponds some money wage rate which is the only way to achieve it

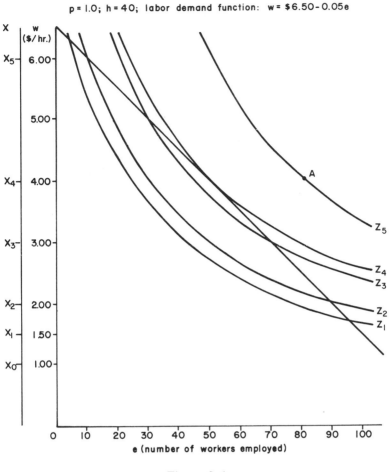

p = 1.0; h = 40; labor demand function: w = \$6.50 - 0.05e

Figure 3-4

when the price index is 1.0, the tax rate zero, and the workweek 40 hours.

Let us take an example and follow it through the several diagrams. In Figure 3-1, when the workweek is 40, the weekly real income per person necessary to achieve X_4 is \$160 (point D), implying a wage rate of \$4 per hour. In Figure 3-2, we observe that with a real income-leisure package yielding a satisfaction of X_4 the employment of 80 workers will place the union on curve Z_5 (point M). In Figure 3-4, the Z curves are the same as those of Figure 3-2, but, having fixed the price level as well as the workweek, we have been able to replace the X's with money wage rates. We see that a wage of $4 and the employment of 80 workers is one of those combinations which would place the union on curve Z_5.

If the union were a wage bill maximizer, each Z would represent a constant wage bill, and we could convert Z readily into monetary units. The vertical scale of Figure 3-3 could be transformed into dollars, and each U_i would consist of combinations of wage bills and strike lengths toward which the union was indifferent. But wage bill maximization, although permitted, is not required by our model and does not, in fact, characterize the union whose preference map appears in Figure 3-4.

With price and tax levels and the workweek still fixed, let us see how the union's range of choice is limited by the fact that it is the employer who determines the number of workers to be hired. The labor demand function identified by the union—and we are supposing it to be correctly identified—shows us the wage-employment combinations which *may* be available. The fact that a wage-employment combination lies on the labor demand curve does not mean that a union can achieve it, but at least it might; whereas points to the right of this curve are out of reach. To each wage rate there corresponds a unique value of e and hence of Z. If we look at the relationship in the other direction, a level of Z may be attainable at one or more wage rates, while many of the higher levels of Z (such as Z_5) have been wiped out of the picture. In Figure 3-4, we have drawn an assumed labor demand function, $w = \$6.50 - 0.05\ e$. Moving along this function, we can find the Z corresponding to each wage rate. The best attainable wage is $4.00, where the demand curve is tangent to Z_4. We shall refer to such tangency points as no-strike optima.

Now, the Z-S indifference diagram of Figure 3-3 can be replaced with a wage-strike length indifference map, valid only so long as the labor demand function remains unchanged. In Figure 3-5, the U's are the same levels of satisfaction as those shown in Figure 3-3. The Z's can now be equated with wage rates read from the demand curve on Figure 3-4.

Since our union prefers shorter strikes to longer ones, the point ($S = 0$, $w = \$4$) represents the best possible arrangement. As the strike length increases, the union is worse off at any given wage rate. At a given strike length, its position worsens the further it moves away from $4.00 in either direction. From Figure 3-4 we see also that the union is indifferent between wage rates of $5.00 and $3.00 (the labor

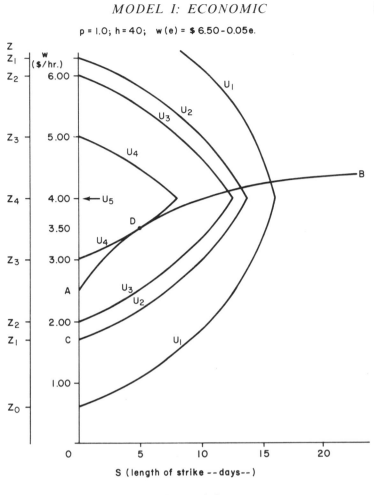

Figure 3-5

demand curve crosses Z_3 at both); hence, for any given strike length, these must lie on the same indifference curve and, from Figure 3-3, we see that with S equal to zero they must lie on U_4. Thus the shape of the map in Figure 3-5 is derived from the shapes of the preceding union preference maps and of the labor demand curve; the employment constraint is built in.

The strike length function further restricts the union's choice. Figure 3-5 shows those combinations of wage rates (with implied levels of Z) and strike lengths which are conceivable once the restriction imposed by the labor demand curve is taken into account. But most of the points on this graph will be irrelevant to the union's decision, for in the majority of cases the horizontal coordinate of the point will stand for a strike which is either shorter or longer than necessary to achieve the wage rate in question. Earlier, we saw that one cannot suppose an $S(Z)$ function with a unique strike length corresponding to each level of Z. But with $h, p, t,$ and $e(w)$ given, a unique relationship from wage rates to strike lengths emerges. $S(w)$ stipulates the (mininum) length of strike necessary to achieve each wage rate.

The market supply curve (a third constraint which has not entered our analysis previously) establishes the minimum rate at which the employer could obtain the quantity of labor demanded by him. Above this minimum there may be a range of rates he would grant without taking a strike; beyond this range, progressively larger values of w can be obtained with progressively longer strikes; the curve here has a positive and finite slope. But there is some wage which is the maximum attainable—the employer would go out of business rather than grant more—and here the curve becomes a horizontal line.

It seems worth emphasizing that $S(w)$ shows employer willingness to take a strike, while the union's willingness to engage in a work stoppage is indicated by the slopes of the curves marked U in Figure 3–5. The smaller are these slopes, the more strike-prone is the union.

CAB in Figure 3-5 is a strike length ($S(w)$) function. There will be some wage rate at which the market supply curve and the employer's labor demand curve intersect. The employer will not wish to go below this wage, which we have arbitrarily assumed to be $1.70 (point C). The maximum attainable wage is about $4.50. The union is restricted to points on CAB. Furthermore, points with wages above the no-strike optimum of $4.00 may be ignored, since they are inferior to other points on CAB below $4.00.

Where AB touches U_4 is the union's optimum: a wage rate of $3.50 obtained after a strike of five days (point D). By noting the indices of the indifference curves which cross AB at various wage rates, we can compile the union's preference ordering in this situation. Thus, $3.50 is preferred to $4.00, the no-strike optimum. In turn, $4.00 is preferred to $2.00; the union is indifferent between $2.00 and $4.10, both of which lie on curve U_3 and are inferior to the alternatives on CAB between them, and so on. In our illustration, the employer's relative willingness to resist, combined with the union's relative unwillingness to strike, leads the latter to a lower optimum wage than would be the case if fear of unemployment were the sole constraint, but this need not be so. Either a steeper $S(w)$ curve (implying less employer resistance) or gentler U curves (implying greater union militance) could move the tangency point to $4.00, but no higher. And with a gentler $S(w)$ curve retaining its original intercept and/or steeper U curves, the union's optimum could fall to $2.50 (with no strike), but not lower.

The no-strike optimum ($4.00 in our example) does not necessarily represent the outcome of the bargaining nor, as we have seen, the union's preferred wage. It is an upper limit beyond which neither party wishes to go; the result of negotiations will be at or below it. But the final optimum ($3.50 after a strike of five days in our example) is not only the union's first choice but is also the bargaining outcome so long as our union forms its preferences in an environment of certainty. Given the available alternatives, which it knows, it will be best off if it strikes for five days and thereby achieves a wage rate of $3.50. In later chapters, uncertainty will enter our scheme, and probability distributions will replace the labor demand and strike length functions. Then, the union's final optimum will no longer be the necessary result of the bargaining process.

But for the time being, a slight "unofficial" relaxation of our assumptions may make this model seem more relevant to many readers. Real unions, like real people, do not know the future precisely, but they do form expectations about it. The labor demand and strike length functions may be viewed as the union's (single-valued) expectations about the employment and strikes attached to different wage rates. The union forms its preferences (and its policy) on the basis of these expectations, which may, of course, turn out to have been quite wrong. A union which believes its world to be the one pictured in Figure 3-5 will go on strike in the hope of getting $3.50 rather than settle now for $2.50.

Figure 3-6 is a three-dimensional portrayal of the union utility function shown in Figure 3-5. The peak is at a wage of $4.00 and no strike. The ridge at this wage represents the highest utility achievable at each strike length. But the union must follow the path CAB, representing the strike length function, and it maximizes its utility by climbing to the highest elevation on this path. Path and ridge may cross, as they do in Figure 3-6. This crossing may or may not represent the best position from the union's viewpoint. In our example, it does not: beyond point D, corresponding to the tangency of U_4 and AB in Figure 3-5, the path leads downhill.

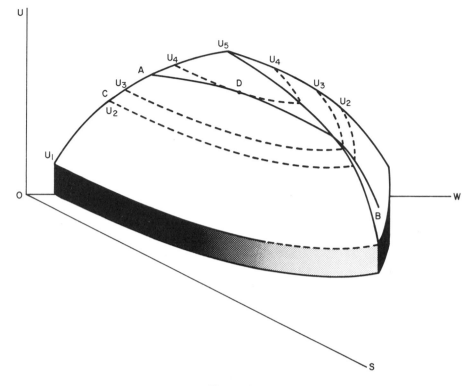

Figure 3-6

We have now presented a model of a union which is interested in the real income, leisure, and employment enjoyed by its members. It is limited in its demands by the desire to avoid "too long" a strike and "too much" unemployment. With $p,t,$ and h fixed, our union had a preference ordering over all conceivable combinations of values of $w,e,$ and S. By making both e and S functions of w, most of these combinations were removed from consideration, and the union's ordering of the remainder was altered. The one novel element in this model is the incorporation of union attitudes and expectations about strikes in the theory of union preference formation. The strike length function is similar if not identical to the union's idea of Hicks' employers' concession curve, but used in a different context.[9] Recognition of the union's own balancing of prospective wage gains against strike losses

[9] Hicks, *The Theory of Wages,* pp. 141–143.

parallels Ross's emphasis of the importance of the membership's "degree of inclination to strike," but has not previously been incorporated into formal theories concerned with the bargainers' formulations of their goals, as distinguished from theories of the negotiating process itself.

Let us now suppse that the price level were to rise while everything else remained the same, and observe the effects upon our union's preference map. Since our union is interested in real income, the Z-curves in Figure 3-4 would drift upward. A 50% increase in (consumers') prices, for example, would imply that the same satisfaction formerly obtained with a money wage of $4.00 would now require one of $6.00, employment remaining the same. If the selling price of the employer's output also rose by 50%, then the labor demand and Z-curves would move upward by equal (vertical) amounts at each employment level, becoming steeper as they did so. (The labor demand curve is also the curve of the marginal revenue product of labor, and an increase of selling price implies an increase of marginal revenue product in the same proportion.) In this instance, both the set of attainable *real* wage-employment combinations and the utility resulting from each would remain the same.

However, if the selling price of the output remained the same or increased by less than the consumers' price index, so that labor demand did not rise in the same proportion as the Z-curves, the union would be worse off. Some Z's would no longer be attainable. The no-strike optimum might change in either direction or remain the same but, in any case, would yield less satisfaction. An increase in the personal income tax rate would produce a similar result.

Turning now to the effects on the final optimum pictured in Figure 3-5, let us consider first the case where a general price increase has led to proportional movements in the Z- and labor demand curves. The U-curves will drift upward to maintain the same preference relations between real wages and strike lengths. (In the case of our 50% rise in p, the U_5 point would now be at $6.00 instead of $4.00, with S equal to zero.) The position of the *final* optimum would remain the same in real terms if the ordinates of the strike length function AB also rose by 50%. We have not presented a theory of the determination of this function, but if all costs and prices rose by equal proportions this might happen.

However, suppose that the source of disturbance is a tax increase, or a rise in the general price level which does not extend fully to the employer's own output. Suppose also that the strike length function as well as the labor demand curve remain unaltered. In Figure 3-5, a lower Z now attaches to each money wage rate because the real disposable income implied by each money wage has fallen. The U-curves move to the left and some higher levels of U disappear from the graph, having become impossible to achieve whatever the strike length function. The final optimum may change or remain the same, but the utility which it yields will be less than before.

We shall soon see that the addition of one more element to our theory yields the prediction that a worsening of real income will shift the union's final optimum to one involving a longer strike than it would have wished to undertake before the change in income occurred. First, however, we shall explore the effects of a change in the workweek on our present model.

Variations in h will shift the preference maps of Figures 3-4 and 3-5, but we cannot say *a priori* whether an increase in the workweek will enhance or diminish the satisfaction enjoyed from a particular wage-employment combination. Basically, this is because an increase in the workweek implies a rise in income at the expense of leisure, and our unionists may or may not regard the gain as adequate compensation for the loss. Figures 3-1 and 3-4 can be used to illustrate. Both show that a 40-hour workweek and weekly income of $80 (wage rate of $2) place our union on utility level X_2. In Figure 3-1, this is point B. The straight line JK connects all the weekly incomes which, varying the workweek, can be obtained at a wage of $2 per hour. The fact that JK is tangent to curve X_2 at B indicates that a 40-hour week is viewed by the union as optimal at this wage rate. In this case, either a rise or fall in the workweek with no change in the wage would leave the membership worse off; in one case, the extra money would not be worth the added effort, while in the other direction the extra leisure would be insufficient to compensate for the reduction in income. Returning to Figure 3-4, where a wage of $2.00 is now equated with X_2, either a shorter or a longer workweek would place this wage on a lower indifference curve. But this is not true of all wage rates. Consider a wage of $6 per hour, implying when $h = 40$ a weekly income of $240 and utility level X_5 (point H in Figure 3-1). Line LK in the same diagram connects the weekly incomes which various workweeks would yield at this wage. A moderate reduction of the workweek would leave the union better off while any increase would worsen its position.

Sometimes, a reduction in the workweek is accompanied by a decline in the average wage rate, even though the negotiated wage remains the same. This is the case if the average wage is compounded of a straight time wage for a certain number of hours and a premium wage for the remainder. Should overtime be reduced or eliminated, both the workweek and the average wage fall. This may leave the workers either better or worse off. Examples of both possibilities can be found in Figure 3-1, if we interpret wage lines such as *JK* as representing average rates. Starting at point *B,* there is no way to reduce both the workweek and the average money wage without impairing the workers' situation. If we start at points *C* or *H* instead, it is possible to accompany a reduction of the workweek with a mild wage cut and move the workers to a higher utility level.

We shall now add to our theory the concept of the "target zone." Briefly, there may be one or more wage rates, weekly real income levels, levels of employment, etc., for the getting or keeping of which the union and its members will give up a great deal (of employment, leisure, strike time, etc.). In Figures 3-1, 3-4, and 3-5 the slopes of the indifference curves show us rates at which the union and its members are willing to exchange one source of satisfaction for another. In Figure 3-1, the trade-off is between real income and leisure, and in 3-4 between wages and employment. Figure 3-5 shows the unionists' willingness to incur the losses and discomforts attendant upon a strike in order to gain higher wages, given their wage-employment preferences and the demand for labor. As the graphs are drawn, these rates of substitution change rather gently. But many economists have suggested in effect that at some point or within some narrow range the slopes of at least some of these curves may change quite markedly. What has evidently impressed all of these writers have been observations that unions are sometimes prepared to make quite substantial sacrifices of employment, of time on strike, or of both in order to get or retain some particular wage rate or level of income. In times of depression, a union may risk its existence by striking to defend an established wage in the teeth of widespread unemployment and a depleted treasury; in periods of prosperity it may wage a militant battle to restore parity with some other union which has won a substantial increase. In both cases as well as others, the idea of a sharp change in the slope of its wage-employment or wage-strike length indifference curves in the neighborhood of the target wage is suggested. Except in the relatively rare instances when the workweek is in dispute, what the union is pursuing or defending so vigorously will at least appear to be the money wage rate. And appearance may conform to reality, or the union's underlying objective may be some real income level, or level of satisfaction from income and employment.

Cartter, as we have seen, posits that the typical union will sacrifice a large amount of employment rather than take less than the current wage.[10] In his wage-employment map, the region around the current rate is a target zone. Hicks emphasizes union willingness to endure a long strike in order to win some target wage. "There is some level of wages to which in particular the men consider themselves entitled. In order to secure this level they will stand out for a long while, but they will not be much concerned to raise wages above it."[11] Writing at a time when British unions had recently been much concerned with resisting wage cuts, Hicks emphasized the current rate as target but did not exclude other possibilities.

> When the dispute arises originally out of the men's claim for an advance, a horizontal stretch (i.e. a range of wage rates over which the unionists will accept much additional strike time in return for a slightly higher wage—wna) is indeed less likely; but even in this case, some new level may easily invoke a special attachment—because it has been granted elsewhere, and is therefore considered fair, or because it has been paid at some earlier period, or for some similar reason.[12]

Ross's discussion, quoted on page 25 above, of the conditions under which rank-and-file pressure on union leadership is "likely to be imperative" suggests that the target is some level of real income. Unlike Hicks, Ross was writing in an environment in which money wage cuts were rare. As causes of membership militance, he mentions inflation in the price level and reductions in take-home pay. (With respect to the latter, wartime tax increases and postwar reductions in hours, especially overtime, come to mind.) Since the other major circumstance which makes for militance according to Ross is an invidious comparison of the membership's own wages with those of other groups of workers, his version of the union's target may be interpreted as a ratio of disposable real income per member in "our" union to that enjoyed by members of another.

Also cited earlier was Pen's observation of "the very real fact that unions are sometimes prepared to make great sacrifices for a wage increase of a few cents" after which "a further wage increase . . . is hardly valued at all."[13]

---

[10] Allan M. Cartter, *Theory of Wages and Employment* (Homewood, Ill.: Irwin, 1959), pp. 90–91.

[11] Hicks, *The Theory of Wages*, p. 143.

[12] *Ibid.*, p. 153.

[13] Pen, *The Wage Rate Under Collective Bargaining*, p. 58.

Such abrupt changes in marginal rates of substitution along indifference curves have important implications for trade union behavior, and seem to be worth introducing into our model. We need a general name for them. "Kink" will not quite do, since it is associated with the kinked demand curves which oligopolists are said to face; the slopes of these are always discontinuous at the kink. The changes in our slopes may or may not be discontinuous; it is required only that they be substantial over a small range. We shall call these zones of abrupt change "target zones" because they are associated with target levels of the wage rate, real income, etc. By not insisting on actual discontinuities, we open the possibilities of targets which are ranges rather than points and of ranges which are more target-like than others.

The target variable may be the wage rate, the workweek, or the level of employment. There may be target levels of satisfaction from income and leisure (X) or from income, leisure, and employment (Z). A target zone may represent some level of satisfaction currently enjoyed, or a peak level once enjoyed but later lost. It could be a contract containing $x\%$ more income or equivalent compensation than the previous one, or an agreement regarded as yielding an equitable relationship with the satisfactions achieved by some other group of workers. And among the possible connotations of equity are both the maintenance of some traditional wage difference and the elimination of such a difference when it runs against one's own group.

Earlier, we saw that if "utility" depends on parameters outside the union's power as well as on the negotiated money wage and workweek, then a change in one of these parameters will alter the union's indifference map. However, our analysis gave us no reason to suppose that such changes in parameters would lead in any systematic way to changes in the no-strike optimum wage, the final optimum wage, or the employment and strike lengths associated respectively with these optima. We predicted only that a worsening of the parameters would leave the union worse off at each money wage rate.

But with the concept of target zones included in our model, we can predict that very often (although not always) the worsening of a parameter will raise both optimum money rates, reduce the employment associated with the no-strike optimum, and increase the length of strike associated with the final optimum. In the case of a Ross-type union whose members' utilities depend on the ratio of their own real incomes to those of other workers, a rise in real incomes of members of union B would have the same effects on union A as would the reduction of A's own real incomes.

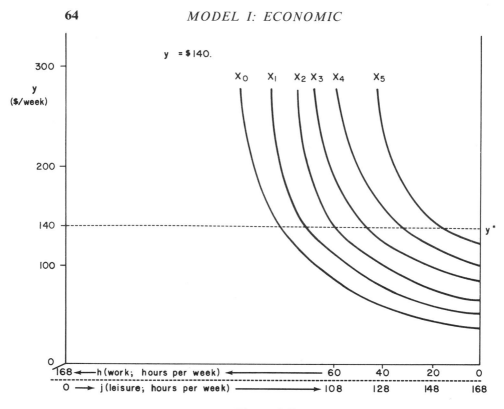

Figure 3-7

Figures 3-7 through 3-9 are preference maps of a union with a target real disposable income, y^*, of \$140 weekly. Just *why* this is a target is not specified; it might be current real income, a past peak, the level achieved by some other group, etc. At incomes above \$140, the income-leisure indifference (X-) curves of the union shown in Figure 3-7 are the same as those of the union depicted in Figure 3-1; below \$140, the relatively small slopes of Figure 3-7 reflect the union members' unwillingness to accept any lower income without a very large payment in the form of added leisure. The "rubber axis" diagrams of Figures 3-2 and 3-3 are presumed to be still valid.

Once again, we shall assume h to be given as 40, p as 1.0, and t as zero, and infer the union's preference map over wage rates and employment. The target y of \$140 implies a target hourly money wage, w^*, of \$3.50. The resulting preference map in Figure 3-8 follows completely from our new income-leisure map (3-7) and the unaltered X-employment map (3-2). Above \$3.50, the indifference curves in 3-8 are

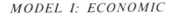

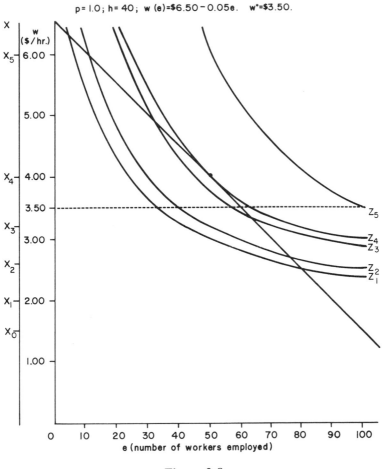

Figure 3-8

identical to those of Figure 3-4. Below w^*, however, a higher money wage is required to achieve any given level of X than was formerly the case. Consequently, the Z-curves are "pushed up"; in this zone, the union will accept a greater loss of employment in return for a higher wage than it would have done in the situation portrayed in Figure 3-4.

The change in our union's willingness to trade time on strike for higher wages is shown in Figure 3-9, which is derived from Figures 3-8 and 3-3. Again, the curves are flatter below the target rate. The union appears to be more strike-prone than the union of Figure 3-5, and in a sense it is. Both unions, however, are equally willing to strike to obtain

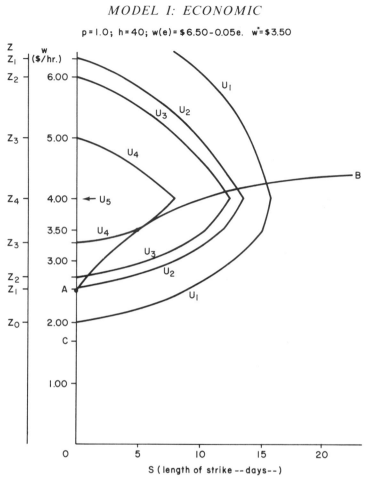

$p = 1.0;\ h = 40;\ w(e) = \$6.50 - 0.05e.\ \ w^{*} = \$3.50$

Figure 3-9

a given degree of satisfaction from wages, employment, and leisure. The more militant stance shown in 3-9 stems from the fact that, once the target is introduced, higher wages are necessary (below \$3.50) to attain any particular satisfaction (Z-) level.

As Figures 3-8 and 3-9 are drawn, the no-strike optimum is \$4.00 with employment of 50, and the final optimum is \$3.50 with $S = 5$. (These are the same outcomes which appear in Figures 3-4 and 3-5.) Now, let us suppose that the withholding tax rate is increased from zero to $16\frac{2}{3}\%$, while the labor demand and strike length functions are unchanged. The hourly money wage necessary to yield the real dis-

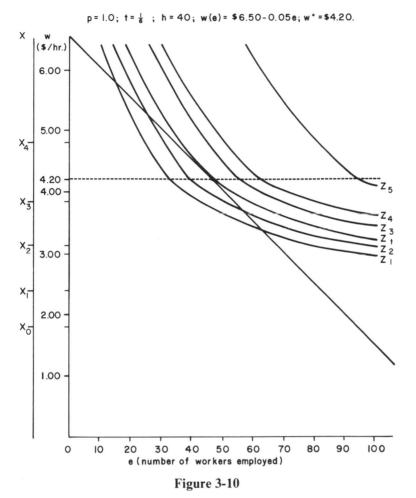

p = 1.0; t = $\frac{1}{6}$; h = 40; w(e) = $6.50 - 0.05e; w* = $4.20.

Figure 3-10

posable target wage of $3.50 now rises from $3.50 to $4.20. ($3.50 is five-sixths of $4.20.) As they did in our earlier example where there was no target zone, the Z-curves drift upward. The result of this drift is shown in Figure 3-10. Z_4, the level of utility at the old tangency point, is now out of reach. The new no-strike optimum is at the target wage of $4.20 with employment of forty-six workers. In Figure 3-11, we observe that the U-curves have drifted to the left. The basic utility function, $U = U(Z,S)$ is the same, but the tax increase has caused the Z obtainable at each point on the labor demand curve to fall. The new relationship between Z and the money wage obtained from Figure

3-10 plus the unaltered relationship among U, Z, and S pictured in Figure 3-3 enable us to plot the new wage-strike length preference map of Figure 3-11. The no-strike optimum yielding $U = U_l$ appears as the point ($S = 0$, $w = \$4.20$), but is not on the strike length function OAB. Restoration of the real target wage (but at a lower utility because of less employment and a longer strike) is within our union's power. And had we flattened its income-leisure (X) curves and hence its Z- and U-curves a bit more to make our union even more militant than it is, the target wage of $\$4.20$, which can be achieved after a strike of thirteen days, would have been the final optimum. But as the graphs are drawn this is not the case, and our union will prefer to settle for a wage of $\$3.80$, which can be had after a strike of only eight days (the tangency point, D, in Figure 3-11).

While the numerical results of our example depend upon the particular wages, etc., chosen, the directions in which the optima move do not. If the initial optima lie between the old and new target money rates, we may expect that a reduction in the utility attached to each money wage will raise both the no-strike and final optima, reduce the employment associated with the former, and increase the strike length involved with the latter.

If we consider the wage-employment trade-off first, an increase in w^* causes the Z-curves to drift upward vertically. As they do so, the slope of any Z-curve at each point between the old and new target rates declines in absolute value. The no-strike optimum is defined as the point where the slopes of the labor demand function and of some Z-curve are equal. After the target rate rises, the slope of the Z-curve at the old optimum will now be (in absolute terms) less than that of the labor demand function. Since along any Z-curve the slope rises as employment falls, the new tangency point must lie at a higher wage and lower employment than the old.

We turn now to the less familiar wage-strike length map. It will be recalled that the U-curves (as in Figure 3-11) connect wage-strike length combinations among which the union is indifferent and that we have assumed that the slope of each such curve rises as we move to the right. The $S(w)$ function, showing the possibilities open to the union, has been drawn so that its slope falls as we move to the right, but our conclusions would follow so long as its slope were positive and finite. When the target money wage rises, the U-curves "flatten" (their slopes fall) in the range between the old and new targets. If the old final optimum lies in this range, then the slope of the U-curve at this old optimum becomes smaller than that of $S(w)$. To find the new

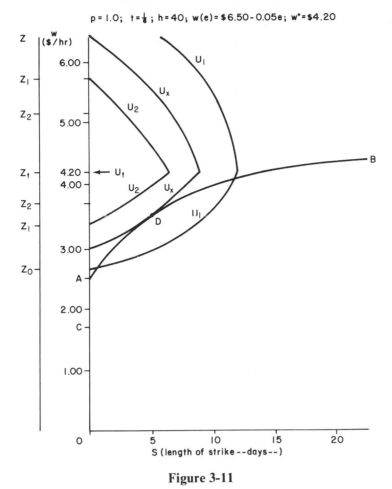

$p = 1.0; \ t = \frac{1}{8}; \ h = 40; \ w(e) = \$6.50 - 0.05e; \ w^* = \$4.20$

Figure 3-11

optimum, where some U has a slope as large as that of $S(w)$, we must move to the right, to a higher wage and longer strike.

There is an exception: if the slopes of the U-functions near the vertical axis are larger than that of the $S(w)$ curve both before and after they have been "flattened" by the rise in the target wage, then the final optimum will remain unaltered at the highest wage which can be achieved without a strike.

The foregoing is a *ceteris paribus* analysis which supposes that the events which raise the target money wage do not affect the labor demand and strike length functions. Hence, it will have little relevance to an economy-wide inflation which affects the selling prices of all types of output and the demand for inputs in about the same way. It will be more appropriate when a rise in consumers' prices is not matched by increased demand for labor inputs, or when reductions in take-home disposable income stem from higher taxes or from cuts in overtime.

Our concept of the target zone is similar to that underlying the near-kinks in Cartter's union indifference maps, but accommodates other variables besides wages and employment. By endowing our union with both target zones and an orientation toward real income, we have been able to predict that a worsening of income-affecting parameters beyond the union's control will increase its willingness to sacrifice employment and time on strike in order to regain at least some of the ground it has lost. Finally, by expanding the domain of union A's utility function to include the wage rates achieved by union B, and then positing a "target" at some accustomed difference of wage rates between the two, our framework provides a theoretical basis for claiming that wage-rounds may be transmitted by interunion emulation as well as by competition in product and labor markets.

Our model of the "concordant and certain" union is now complete. The next task will be to remove some of the unrealistic assumptions which provided helpful rough scaffolding during the construction of the model, and to replace them with other suppositions truer to the actual edifice we seek to imitate.[14]

---

[14] A preliminary version of much of this chapter and of the following one was presented at the Forty-First Annual Conference of the Western Economic Association in 1966. An abstract appears in *Western Economic Journal*, V: 1 (December 1966), pp. 99–100.

Chapter IV

INTERMEDIATE MODEL II:
POLITICO-ECONOMIC

In the recent history of attempts to frame general explanations of the behavior of unions as labor market representatives of their constituents' interests, there has been a dichotomy of approach. The formulators of wage-employment preference models gave no formal consideration to possible divergence of preferences within the union. On the other hand, Ross emphasized differences between organizational and membership goals as well as the importance of pressure from the rank and file, but did not develop a formal model. The practice emerged of labeling these two approaches, respectively, "economic" and "political." Relatively little attention was devoted to attempting to combine them. Berkowitz, however, starts with the explicit assumption that a union, as a "seller . . . of memberships in the organization" which must have "some regard for the costs involved," has certain interests of its own; and his analysis uses an "economic" maximand (net revenue) subject to a "political" constraint (the union must retain the allegiance of a majority of the workers whom it represents).[1] Lester regards the two approaches as complementary and presents a "theoretical formulation . . . that draws on both political and economic interpretations" but stops short of that "refinement of the model" which "would be required to convert it into a specific set of propositions formulated with sufficient rigor to permit mathematical manipulation or experimental verification."[2] And Ashenfelter's and Johnson's bargaining theory, as we have noted, starts with the explicit assumption that three parties are involved: a profit-actuated firm, a survival-seeking union leadership, and a wage-oriented rank and file.[3]

In this chapter, we shall incorporate internal differences into the model constructed in Chapter III. Two types of differences will be considered. First, we shall take up some disparities between goals of

[1]Berkowitz, "The Economics of Trade Union Organization and Administration," *Industrial and Labor Relations Review,* Vol. 7 (July 1954), p. 575.

[2]Richard A. Lester, *Economics of Labor* (second edition, New York: The Macmillan Company, 1964), p. 155.

[3]Ashenfelter and Johnson, "Bargaining Theory, Trade Unions, and Industrial Strike Activity," *American Economic Review,* LIX (March 1969), pp. 36–39.

the leadership and those of its constituents. Second, we shall explore various implications of conflicts of interest within the membership itself.

Up to this point, these problems of internal discord have been avoided by supposing that all members of a union, including its leaders, have identical goals. For a few pages more, we shall retain the assumption that the members share a common preference map of the form:[4]

$$U = U\left[\frac{wh(1 - t)}{p}, j, e, S\right].$$

This will allow us to concentrate on the idea that the union has some institutional interests of its own. These institutional goals may be referred to, also, as leadership goals. They should not, however, be regarded as reflections only of the personal tastes of the leaders as individuals. They include objectives which are related to the survival and growth of the union as an institution and toward which any leaders, having assumed office, might be expected to devote some effort. Like Berkowitz, we shall presume that the union desires to retain or acquire the right to act as the workers' bargaining representative and, once that is done, to maximize net revenue. Berkowitz' analysis treats the provision of "service" in general to the membership and does not deal specifically with the formulation of wage policy, but we can apply his approach to this problem within our framework.

The meaning of "net revenue" with respect to a union is not self-evident. What we mean is the excess of gross revenues over the costs of providing some accustomed level of services to current members. Berkowitz calls these "costs of administration" and lists the following:

1. The costs of collective bargaining—including the negotiation of the agreement, the processing of complaints and grievances arising under its terms, and the costs of strikes to secure and enforce the agreement.

2. Costs involved in the collection of revenues, record-keeping, maintenance of seniority lists, processing applications for memberships, transfers, etc.

3. The costs of providing services other than collective bargaining—such as legal aid, political action, union counseling,

[4] The symbols are defined on pages 45–46, above.

participation in community activities, athletic and recreational programs, etc.

4. Costs of educational and promotional activities designed to maintain the unit as a functioning part of the union. These include the expenses of persuading new hires to join the union and of persuading others to retain their union membership. Even if a union security clause is obtained, promotional costs are still necessary, since the threat of decertification is always present at the expiration of a collective bargaining agreement.[5]

(We enter the qualification that the services listed in the third category should be interpreted as levels of service provided by existing programs.) An excess of revenues over these costs will be called "net revenue." Unions and their leaders typically have objectives beyond the retention of current bargaining rights, and their accomplishment usually requires money. This applies to organizing drives, the provision of new services to members, community action programs, or building homes for retired members, just as it does to the enjoyment of leadership conferences in Honolulu or Miami Beach.

We shall now insert into our model a leadership interested in retaining bargaining rights and, subject to that constraint, in maximizing net revenue. Figure 4-1 shows a wage-strike length indifference map with the workweek, price level, and withholding tax rate given as before. It will be recalled that the labor demand curve and the workers' wage-employment and income-leisure preferences are taken into account, although hidden from view. The no-strike optimum is $4.00. There is a target at $3.00. ABF is the strike length function and the membership's final optimum lies at its tangency with U_5 at point D.

Some level of U, called U^*, represents the minimal level of satisfaction (from real income, leisure, employment and length of strike) at which a critical percentage of the workers will become (or remain) affiliated with the union and thereby assure its survival as bargaining representative. The size of this critical percentage as well as the precise meaning of "affiliation" will, like Dunlop's concept of membership, depend upon the institutional context. Thus, when bargaining rights are decided under the rules used by the National Labor Relations Board in its representation elections, "affiliation"

---

[5] Berkowitz, "The Economics of Trade Union Organization and Administration," p. 583.

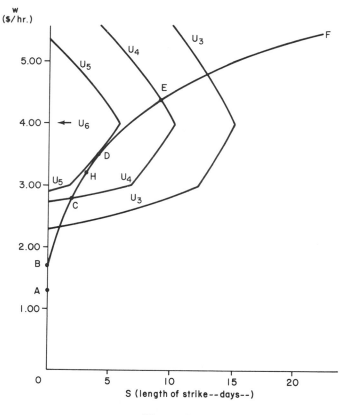

Figure 4-1

will mean "voting for the union," and—ignoring abstainers—U^* will be the minimum level of satisfaction at which at least 50% plus one of the workers will vote for the union. In a system of industrial relations in which the acquisition of bargaining rights depended upon ability to close an enterprise for a certain length of time, "affiliation" would consist of walking a picket line; the "critical percentage" would be the number of pickets required to force closing of the firm.

In Figure 4-1, we shall assume U^* to be U_4 and suppose that the type of affiliation involved is willingness of over half of the workers to support the union in an N.L.R.B.-type representation election. It can be seen that this survival constraint limits the union's choice to points on *CE*. Within this range, there is some wage which maximizes the union's net revenue. (While there could be more than one such wage, we shall suppose it to be unique.) We shall call this wage the institutional optimum.

In order to find maximum net revenue, we must investigate the paths of the union's gross revenues and costs as one moves along ABF toward higher wages and longer strikes. Whether or not strike benefits are paid, a work stoppage drains a union's treasury. Hence, as the wage rises above the maximum attainable without a strike (point B in Figure 4-1), and S increases, so do total costs. Supposing that all revenues come from dues collected from employed members and that individual dues are independent of the wage rate, we must have some assumptions about dues-paying behavior if we are to find the relationship of gross revenues to wages and strike lengths. As the wage rises and employment consequently declines, *potential* gross revenues fall. If the union, once recognized, is assured of a union shop with as close to a compulsory checkoff as the law permits, then potential and actual gross revenues are the same.[6] Both gross and net revenues will be maximized at the lowest wage rate consistent with the survival constraint. Because of the employment effect, this may be at a wage even lower than the largest which could be obtained without a strike. At wage rates which require a strike to win, both the employment effect and the cost of striking will reduce net revenue as the wage rises. In any case, the institutional optimum ($2.80 at C in Figure 4-1) will be less than the membership's ($3.50 at point D) unless the two happen to coincide.

Now let us imagine that there is no union security agreement, so that our union's dues revenues depend upon voluntary payments. Since our workers share common preferences with respect to income, leisure, etc., it seems reasonable to extend their unanimity to the polling booth. Achievement of U^* will then assure the favorable ballots of all workers, while failure to achieve it will cause a unanimous negative vote. If we further extend this unanimity to dues-

---

[6] A maximum of financial union security would be provided by a union shop plus compulsory irrevocable dues checkoff. Under this arrangement, all workers must join the union (union shop) and must permit dues to be withheld from their paychecks. Under present U.S. federal law, the union shop is legal except in those states which choose to outlaw it. While the checkoff is permitted, it must be voluntary and revocable at intervals. However, a union may expel a member whose dues are delinquent and then ask (or press) the employer to dismiss him; under a union shop, a worker cannot legitimize failure to pay dues by leaving the union. We shall speak of the union shop with (voluntary) checkoff as if it assured the union's dues income, although it stops slightly short of this. The union shop does give the union a strong claim on dues from all workers while the checkoff shifts most of the cost of collection onto the employer.

paying, the results are the same as those obtained under the compulsory checkoff. But voting for a union's services in an election need not imply a desire to finance them. The former is an almost costless act, but payment of dues reduces the income and assets available to the individual for other uses. The minimum level of satisfaction required to induce voluntary payments will differ among workers, and some, of course, may never contribute. But we may suppose that, if a worker will pay dues at some utility level U_i, he will also pay dues if higher levels are achieved. Then, as we move from \$2.80 to \$3.50 (and from C to D), rising membership utility increases the ratio of dues payers to employed workers. The resulting tendency toward higher revenues may be reinforced by a decline in the costs of dues collections (such as mailings, sound trucks, opportunities foregone by staff members while pressing for payment). But the higher wages which increase membership utility also reduce employment, so—if the unemployed do not pay dues—gross revenues will be maximized somewhere short of the membership optimum. And because of the cost of striking, the wage which maximizes net revenue will be less than (or in the limiting case equal to) that which maximizes gross.

Thus we arrive at the conclusion that the wage at which net revenue is maximized will often be lower and never be higher than the membership's optimum. And the institutional optimum with union security will often be lower and never higher than the same optimum without it. Because this model ignores interdependence among unions, it does not allow for a possibly significant exception to this conclusion. That is the situation in which a local is pushed beyond its own membership optimum by the national union in order to ease resistance to the demands of other locals negotiating with competitors of the first local's employer.

Our conclusion that union security will make union wage policy more moderate is similar to that of Galloway, although reached by a different route.[7] But Berkowitz, who argues that unions must act as if membership were voluntary, might reject it.[8]

But which optimum—the institutional one or the membership's—will be decisive in the determination of wage policy? Left to its own devices, the leadership would be expected to pick the former. But its desires may be thwarted when, as is often the case, proposed settle-

---

[7] Galloway, "The Economics of the Right to Work Controversy," *Southern Economic Journal*, XXXII (January 1966), p. 316.

[8] Berkowitz, "The Economics of Trade Union Organization and Administration," pp. 585–586.

ments must be submitted for approval to a membership referendum. Typically, local agreements require such ratification while regional and national ones do not, but there are plenty of exceptions in both directions.[9] A continuous membership meeting engaged in continuous voting as the proposed wage rose and strike time elapsed would insist upon the membership optimum. But actually the members will be assembled at discrete intervals.

Any wage at or above the membership optimum will be approved, since in this region (arc *DE* in Figure 4-1) further delay will make everyone worse off. But the leaders (who would prefer the institutional optimum at *C*) would not wait so long. A proposed settlement below the membership optimum will be compared with the proposal the members expect next to encounter if they should reject what is now available. Thus, suppose in Figure 4-1 that, after a two-day strike, union and management negotiators reach tentative agreement on the institutional optimum of $2.80. The union then submits this proposal to the membership along with the statement, which is believed, that rejection of the offer will prolong the strike for another thirteen days. The choice is then between $2.80 now or $5.00 after a total of fifteen days out. Since the former alternative is preferred by the members, they will vote to accept. But if the members believe that another offer can be obtained and another referendum held within a week (i.e. before the S-line crosses U_4 again), they will reject the proposal.

As we have shown, the membership optimum wage will ordinarily be larger and never smaller than the institutional optimum, as will the associated strike length. A membership referendum requirement, then, will result in a wage settlement at least as large and normally larger than net revenue considerations alone would dictate.

In the absence of a union shop with checkoff, the paying and withholding of dues could function as a substitute for a membership referendum. One can imagine a membership refusing financial support unless a certain utility level—at the extreme, that associated with the membership optimum wage—were attained. However, refusal of financial support would have to occur before an anticipated unsatisfactory settlement or after an experienced one. An unanticipated settlement could not be prevented by this means. Refusal to pay dues, then, is probably a rather imperfect substitute for the membership referendum. But there is another way in which, espe-

---

[9] Neil W. Chamberlain, *The Labor Sector* (New York: McGraw-Hill, 1956), pp. 221–222.

cially in the absence of required membership ratification of the wage settlement, voting and money may combine to drive the policies of a net revenue maximizing union closer to the membership optimum. Revenues depend upon the level of dues per member as well as on the number who pay them and, as mentioned earlier, an increase in the dues level ordinarily requires a referendum.[10] It seems reasonable to presume that the maximum dues level which the members will impose upon themselves varies directly with the utility obtained from the wage settlement. (The graph of the relationship between wage rate and maximum acceptable dues level may be a step function rather than a smooth curve.) As we move from lower to higher wage rates, increased dues receipts per member may offset the loss of net revenues from reduced employment and a longer strike. With this relation built into the net revenue function, the institutional optimum can lie above the lowest wage needed to assure survival, but still will be below (or, in the limiting case, at) the membership optimum. It is the somewhat unruly membership which "sells" dues increases expensively but *does* have a price which will gain from this possibility; it will be of benefit neither to a local of true loyalists nor to one of inveterate dissenters.

We have added to our basic model a divergence between an institutional objective of maximizing the union's net revenue, presumably characteristic of the leadership, and the aims of the still unanimous rank and file. Unless the two fortuitously coincide, the membership optimum wage will exceed the institutional optimum. The leaders, however, may be forced to compromise with the members by such devices as requirements for ratification of wage settlements which the former propose. One further refinement of the model raises the possibility of compromise in the other direction. The leadership's pursuit of maximum net revenue has been presumed to be relevant within the bounds of a "survival constraint." The desire to maintain the organization may be subject in *its* turn to a net revenue *constraint*.[11] For example, a national union might have no desire to continue representing a group of workers whose local did not at least break even. An unaffiliated local might cease functioning if receipts were so low that leaders had to meet costs out of their own pockets. Thus, we may presume that net revenue maximization operates as the leadership's goal within a representation election survival constraint,

---

[10] Page 23.
[11] Cf. Berkowitz, "The Economics of Trade Union Organization and Administration," p. 591.

which operates in turn within a minimum net revenue constraint. In Figure 4-1, there may be some segment of curve ABF over which net revenue is below the minimum (which might be positive, zero, or negative) at which the organization will continue to function. Suppose that the range of possible outcomes over which it *will* function is ABH, while the survival constraint imposed by the necessity of winning representation elections is still CE. The membership optimum is now (in this example) an impossibility. Referenda or other devices may still raise the wage settlement above the institutional optimum of $2.80 (point C) but only up $3.20 (point H).

From the foregoing we may adduce some conclusions related to public policy which will still hold up after our model has been further complicated by divergent aims among the members, uncertainty, and other concessions to reality. We have seen that a leadership interested in increasing the revenues of the union will be more moderate in its wage demands than the members, because of the employment effect and the cost of striking. The one exception mentioned involves forcing one local beyond its own membership optimum in order to facilitate satisfying other locals in a related product market.[12] If leadership concern for union revenues makes (as we have seen) for restraint in bargaining, it follows that where the aim of public policy is the moderation of union wage demands (whether in order to suppress inflation, or to improve the balance of payments, or to increase the profit share of national income, or to augment savings, etc.), then an appropriate means toward this end lies in increasing the degree to which union leaders can safely disregard the wishes of their constituents.[13] The same conclusion follows if the objective is a reduction in the frequency and duration of strikes. The framers of the Landrum-Griffin Act of 1959 moved in the opposite direction, seeking to make it easier for union members to influence their leaders' conduct in office. Ashenfelter and Johnson found a dummy variable representing this law to be positively and significantly related to strike activity.[14] A step toward augmenting the power of union leadership over its own rank and file would be the repeal of those provisions of

---

[12] Relaxation of our assumption of perfect knowledge of the labor demand and strike length functions on the parts of members and leaders will permit other exceptions. For example, an insecurely organized group of workers might believe rumors that any wage increase would induce a permanent shutdown, while the better-informed leaders were confident that this outcome would not be the case.

[13] Cf. Martin P. Oettinger, "Responsible Democracy or Democratic Irresponsibility," *Financial Analysts' Journal* (March–April 1966), p. 6.

[14] Ashenfelter and Johnson, "Bargaining Theory . . .," p. 47.

this act which require and regulate membership voting on officers, convention delegates, and dues changes, as well as those which limit the right of national unions to impose trusteeships on rebellious locals. The same considerations would logically dictate the legalization of the compulsory, irrevocable checkoff in those sectors of the economy where unions are strongly entrenched, and the complete substitution of private or public mediation and arbitration for N.L.R.B. elections as a means of settling interunion representation disputes. (The writer personally opposes the above proposals, but for reasons unrelated to the present argument.)

We shall now admit into our basic model additonal elements which will convert it into something like the "primarily political institution" responding to "external economic stimuli," which Kerr and Ross described but did not develop formally.[15] We shall allow for heterogeneity of preference orderings among the members, recognizing that people may disagree about wages, hours, employment, and time on strike. For the union which represents them, we shall develop preference orderings based on considerations of institutional and leadership survival. Net revenue maximization will appear only as a subsidiary criterion for choice among alternatives which are equally satisfactory on other grounds. Because this revised model will allow for the possibility that workers dissatisfied with the policies of a union will sometimes leave it, or may never have joined, we can no longer use the terms "workers" and "members" synonymously. We may, however, speak of all the workers as *potential members,* with the understanding that potential union membership *includes those who are already affiliated.*

The potential membership of our union is to be thought of as divided into several groups called *A, B, C,* etc. Within any one group, the members share identical preference orderings over all possible values of (w, h, t, p, e, S). Indeed, this is just what we mean, and *all* that we mean, by the word "group." A group's members need not share other characteristics such as skill, seniority, age, sex, race, current wage, or

---

[15]John T. Dunlop, ed., *The Theory of Wage Determination,* Proceedings of a Conference held by the International Economic Association (London: Macmillan and Co., 1957), p. 387. Kerr described the position of what Professor Roberts had called the "California School" as follows: "It held that trade unions were primarily political institutions which responded both to external economic stimuli and to the external political environment. Externally, the union might be concerned with economics and/or politics, but internally it was politically activated." We are concerned solely with those external stimuli which would ordinarily be classed as "economic," but seek to take account of the union's internal political structure in our analysis.

attitudes toward supervision, although as a practical matter they very well might. All that they *must* have in common to constitute a "group" is their preference ordering over wages, etc.—and their common preference ordering must differ in some respect from that of every other group.

Now an assumption which attributes identical preference orderings to *any* two or more persons may, to some readers, seem as unlikely to fit the facts as our prior supposition that the entire membership of a union would be similarly like- minded. Here it may be pointed out that there is no constraint placed on the size of a "group." Our definition allows for the possibility that there might be as many groups as potential members of a union, with each group counting a single individual in its ranks. We do intend, however, to treat groups as member aggregates, since what concerns us now is the development of a means of approach to the effects of internal division on union policy making. The real phenomenon which our partition into groups is meant to approximate is the organization divided into several blocs. Members of such blocs are apt to have aims which, while not perhaps identical, are nonetheless similar and markedly distinct from the objectives of members of other blocs. By assuming homogeneity of preferences within the groups of our model, we are putting aside the smaller differences in order to concentrate on the larger ones.

Once a union's potential membership is thought of as divided into two or more such groups, we may speak of the (no-strike or final) optimum wage of each group, but no longer of a membership optimum (save in an exceptional case to be mentioned later). At a membership optimum, everyone feels he cannot better his position. But now, what is optimal for Group *A* is suboptimal for Group *B*.

In addition to the group optima, there is in the new situation what we shall call the majority wage. This is a wage such that there is no other single wage rate which a majority of the union's potential members would consider superior to it. So long as we assumed all members to have identical preference orderings, the membership optimum was also the majority wage, and the majority was unanimous. Under our new assumptions, the majority wage will always be the optimum of at least one group, as we shall see. But this group may account for a very small proportion of the total membership, and some other groups may find the majority wage to be quite distasteful.

Furthermore, the majority wage must not be viewed as providing the greatest total satisfaction to the membership. Since our concept of utility does not allow addition, we cannot say what wage this would be. But even if we were to introduce additive utilities into our model, the wage yielding greatest total satisfaction would not necessarily be the majority wage.

A union whose members' preference orderings are not identical is illustrated in Figure 4-2. We continue to suppose that our union deals with a single wage rate rather than a structure. Conflict among group preferences could arise from differences in vulnerability to layoff or from differences in relative willingness to strike. There are three groups in the diagram, *A, B,* and *C.* With *p, h, t,* and the labor demand function given, the *Z-S* preference pattern becomes, as before, a

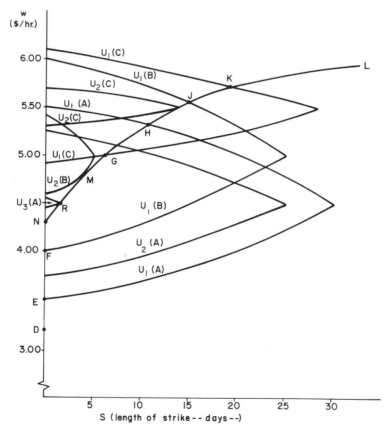

$$U^*(A) = U_1(A); \ U^*(B) = U_1(B); \ U^*(C) = U_1(C)$$

Figure 4-2

wage-strike length indifference map. Figure 4-2 shows two curves from C's map, labeled $U_1(C)$ and $U_2(C)$. $U_2(C)$ is superior to $U_1(C)$. Two similar curves are shown for Group B and three for A. To avoid unneeded complexities, we have omitted target wage rates (except the no-strike optima) but each group might have one or more. Curve *DNL* is the strike length function. The employer would not wish to pay less than $3.20 because the supply of labor would then be inadequate; he would yield up to $4.30 without taking a strike (point N). After a strike of about six days he would yield $5.00 (point G); after 15 days, $5.55 (point J), etc. The curve is asymptotic to a wage of about $6.00; this represents the upper limit toward which the employer could be pushed.

Each group's no-strike optimum (the wage above which it would prefer not to go because of the employment effect) is found at the vertical ordinate where the slopes of its indifference curves change sign (the curves "bend back"). Each group's final optimum wage is found at the point where one of its indifference curves is tangent to the strike length function. Inspection of Figure 4-2 shows that these optima are:

Group	*No-strike Optimum*	*Final Optimum*
A	$4.50	$4.50
B	5.00	4.80
C	5.50	5.50

There would be a membership optimum only if the group preference maps, despite divergences elsewhere, happened to have coincident final optima at some point on *DNL*. But they do not. To find the majority wage, we need to know the relative sizes of the groups. Suppose that any two groups constitute a majority of the membership. The majority wage will then be $4.80, which can be obtained with a strike of four days. This is the point marked M in Figure 4-2. If we move up the strike length function from point D, everyone will prefer to increase the wage until we reach $4.50, which is Group A's final optimum (point R). Further increases at the expense of a longer strike will be endorsed by Groups B and C, but opposed by A, until we reach $4.80. Above $4.80, C would prefer to push still further, but A and B would not. Finally, all groups would oppose going above C's optimum at $5.50.

Hence, $4.80 is the majority wage: there is no other wage which a majority would prefer to it. A higher wage would be championed only by *C,* a lower one would be favored only by *A.*

While the majority wage will prove to be a useful concept, the reader must not think that our union is necessarily committed to achieving it. Once again, we shall assume that our union is concerned with its survival as bargaining representative of the workers in question. Suppose that its survival is threatened by an N.L.R.B. type election involving the whole collection of workers contained in Groups *A, B,* and *C* combined. (Actual N.L.R.B. ballots contain the names of all competing unions as well as the alternative, "no union"; if no entry receives a majority in the first tally, a runoff is held between the two alternatives receiving the largest number of votes. We shall presume our union to be faced with just one serious opponent; it might be another union or "no union.") To win the election requires a majority of votes, and in this particular instance any two or more groups will suffice for that purpose.

Whether the members of a group will opt for or against the incumbent union depends (given the price level and withholding tax rates) upon the wages and hours obtained, the length of strike required to get these, and the level of employment of members of the group which results. Group *A* will vote (unanimously) for the union if and only if the level of *U* its members experience is greater than or equal to some critical level which we shall call $U^*(A)$; there are similar threshold levels for Groups *B* and *C.* From the viewpoint of the survival constraint, all (w,h,p,t,e,S) such that, for two or more groups, $U \geq U^*$ are preferred to all (w,h,p,t,e,S) which fail to meet this condition. In Figure 4-2, suppose that $U^*(A) = U_1(A)$, that $U^*(B) = U_1(B)$, and that $U^*(C) = U_1(C)$. To obtain the votes of at least two of the groups, the union must pick some solution on segment *FJ* of the strike length function; that is, a wage between \$4.00 and \$5.55. Below \$4.00, the votes of Groups *B* and *C* would be cast against it, and it would lose its status as bargaining representative for all groups combined; above \$5.55, the negative votes of *A* and *B* would defeat it. If its preferences are based solely on this survival criterion, the union will be indifferent among wages between \$4.00 and \$5.55.

We shall next take up three supplemental criteria which might determine preferences within this range. The first is net revenue maximization. If a union shop were certain provided the election could be won, the institutional optimum would be the lowest wage at which the union could win, \$4.00 in our example. Between \$4.00 and \$4.30 the union would lose dues and hence revenues because of the employment effect; while to move above \$4.30 it would have to meet strike costs as well. With voluntary membership and dues payment, the optimum cannot be located precisely. For, while higher wages reduce net revenue through the employment effect and strike costs, they may also raise it by increasing the proportion of workers who pay. *If* voting for the union were to imply willingness to pay dues to it, then only in the segment *GH* would all members pay dues. (While *GH* lies above and excludes the majority wage in our example, this need not be the case.) Maximum gross dues revenues would not lie above *H* (where Group *A* quits paying); the employment effect would drive this maximum below *H* and conceivably below *G* (if *C* were a small group and the employment effect quite strong). Because of strike costs, maximum net revenue would lie at a wage below that which maximized gross.

But voting for a union need not imply paying dues to it, and intragroup homogeneity need not extend to dues paying behavior. Two weaker assumptions similar to those used earlier seem reasonable: first, that no one would vote against a union and then pay dues to it; and, second, that as the level of *U* experienced by a group changes in one direction the proportion of dues payers within the group will not move in the opposite way. Strike costs, of course, are still assumed to rise as the strike lengthens. Logically, these suppositions leave us with a set of possible net revenue maxima anywhere in the survival range, with additional possible maxima excluded only because they are not compatible with survival, such as the points on segments *DF* and *JL* in Figure 4-2.

Without a union shop, then, we cannot infer within our model the particular wage rate which maximizes net revenue unless we know the magnitudes of strike costs, the employment effect, and potential members' financial responses to changes in utility. But we can say that the net revenue maximizing union will be especially impelled toward solutions at the low end of the survival range if the employment effect is strong and/or the marginal cost of striking high. Also, differences among groups in dues paying behavior will affect the union's choice within the survival range. Finally, maximum net revenue may be at, above, or below the majority wage. It may lie at some group's final optimum or at none. It will not lie above the highest final optimum, but may fall beneath the lowest.

Once again, concern with net revenue is seen to introduce a bias toward relatively low wage settlements and short strikes into the union's wage policy. If there is a union shop, the effects of this bias will be stronger than if there is not. However, as in the one-group case analyzed earlier, a requirement of membership ratification of dues increases may affect the union leaders' policies much as voluntary dues payment would do.

A second basis for the determination of union policies within the range of outcomes compatible with survival is represented by the practice, discussed above, of submitting proposed settlements for membership ratification or rejection. Such a rule limits the range of options open to the leadership. In the analysis which follows, we shall make the simplifying assumption that all workers whom the union wishes to represent are voting members, whether or not they would favor the union in an N.L.R.B. election or pay dues to it willingly. If the membership votes continuously on a continuously varying proposal beginning at the lowest wage which the employer, taking account of labor supply considerations, would offer (point *D* in Figure 4-2), it would settle at the majority wage. This parallels our earlier finding that such a meeting would adopt the membership optimum in the one-group case. Given our still unrelaxed assumption that the members and leaders of the union have made a correct estimate of the labor demand and strike length functions, the majority wage will always be compatible with union survival if any wage is.

It is more realistic to suppose that there will be no vote until the leadership submits a proposal; and that if this is rejected, some time must elapse before another proposed agreement is submitted. In this case, the solution need not be at *M*. Any proposed wage lying above the majority wage will always be accepted. A proposal to settle for less will, as before, be compared with the proposal the members expect next to encounter if they should reject what is now available. For example, suppose in Figure 4-2 that union and management negotiators reach a tentative agreement on a wage of $4.30, the highest which can be had without a strike, and that the union submits this proposal to the membership along with the statement (which is believed) that its rejection will lead to a strike of at least ten days. The choice is then between taking $4.30 now or voting on $5.30 after ten days on strike. Group *A* will vote to accept. $4.30 leaves them well above $U_2(A)$, while the strike involved in getting $5.30 would drive them almost to $U_1(A)$. Group *C* will vote no. Even $5.30 is short of its optimum and $4.30 is far shorter. The decision is up to Group *B*, whose optimum is between the alternatives.

A union may seek net revenue maximization within the survival constraint but be required to submit proposals to the membership for ratification. If the wage which maximizes net revenue is equal to or greater than the majority wage, the union will strike until it reaches the former and submit this for certain approval. But if net revenue is maximized below the majority wage, the goal may be unattainable. The best the union leaders can then do is to settle for that wage which a majority would accept which promises the highest net revenue.

We conclude that a requirement of membership ratification will increase the likelihood that the settlement will lie close to the majority wage.

A third possible criterion for choice within the survival range is this: in an N.L.R.B. election, the union might wish to obtain a unanimous vote of approval (or, if this is precluded, the largest possible vote) and thus discourage future raids from rival unions or hopes for eventual decertification on the part of the employer. Such a policy might be sensible even though achieving such a result might leave a majority of the membership worse off than a solution yielding a smaller pro-union percentage. The reason is that the number of "yes" and "no" votes can be easily ascertained by outsiders, but the closeness of each voter's decision cannot. In our example, points on GH would be preferred in this case to all others. While this segment happens to lie entirely above the majority wage, this need not be so.

Let us return our attention to the union's basic problem of survival in the face of divergences of preferences among its constituents. Where the union's survival depends upon the results of an N.L.R.B.-type election, the union must pick a bargaining outcome sufficiently satisfactory to groups representing a majority of the electorate that they will vote in the union's favor. There may be a broad range of such solutions, as in Figure 4-2, or there may be few or none. Each group is presumed to have a threshold level of satisfaction, U^*, at which its vote changes from "no" to "yes." This concept needs closer examination. Because we shall use U^* in several models in this and later chapters, the following discussion sometimes goes beyond the bounds of the particular model with which we have just been concerned.

The points on U^* represent conditions which are barely good enough to entice the group to affiliate (in a sense depending on the context); the points just below U^* are just bad enough to provoke disaffiliation. Involved in the group's decision to affiliate or not are the potential benefits and costs to be gained from each alternative. These will include wages and job security, and whatever additional positive or negative satisfactions are expected from being a union member rather than not, or a member of one union rather than of another. The more attractive alternative Y appears to a group, the higher will be the threshold level of utility necessary to induce its (new or continued) affiliation with alternative X. When the managers of alternatives compete effectively, threshold utilities rise and the range of solutions compatible with the survival of the incumbent alternative is narrowed.

The relative attractiveness of alternatives may be affected by the possibility that the loser will retaliate. Suppose that a group of workers otherwise inclined to replace Union X with Union Y fear that, once ousted, X would used secondary boycotts to reduce the market for its employer's products and thus reduce the incomes of members of the group. The group's U^* for X will now be relatively lower than in the absence of the threatened reprisal. Or suppose that the plant is nonunion and the choice is between continuing in this fashion and choosing Union X as bargaining agent. A rumor that the employer will shut down in the event of a union victory will raise the level of expected satisfaction necessary to induce affiliation with X. (U^* for affiliation with X will be higher; U^* for continued "affiliation" with nonunion status will be lower.)

Another element which will affect threshold utility levels is the effort required to shift affiliation from one alternative to another. This is a sort of transfer cost. When workers can make a choice between two established unions in a secret ballot election conducted on the premises by the N.L.R.B., the cost of shifting affiliation is quite small; alternatives are readily available. U^*'s may then be relatively high, and the contestants forced to perform quite satisfactorily for their present or potential constituents. But if a group of workers wishing to oust an incumbent union yet desirous of continuing collective bargaining must start from scratch to set up a rival organization, the costs of doing this are thrown into the balance. This is true, as well, of hitherto unorganized workers who wish to set up a union but do not attract the interest of an existing one. In either case, U^* for continuation of the present situation is lower than it would be if an established rival were in the picture. Many of the costs of establishing a new alternative are monetary; others involve giving up present uses of leisure time in order to work in organizing. Still others require a very broad interpretation of the idea of "cost." For example, a group of near-illiterates speaking different languages and lacking experience in running any type of voluntary association will find the effort of self-organization to be very difficult. And so would a group of well-educated and competent female employees reared in a culture which had taught them that it was wrong and unladylike to assert self-interest or to quarrel with established authority.

As the above remarks suggest, both public law and the private rules of trade union federations can affect substantially both the availability and the attractiveness of alternatives. Traditionally, in the days before the Wagner Act, the American Federation of Labor sought to prevent and mediate both representational and jurisdictional disputes among its affiliates.[16] Since the AFL-CIO merger, the Federation has developed a mechanism whereby both types of disputes are submitted to mediators drawn from outside the ranks of organized labor, and then if necessary to outside umpires who may make binding decisions subject to appeal to the AFL-CIO Executive Council, which may initiate sanctions against violators.[17] This machinery handled 918 cases between January 1, 1962, and August 31, 1969.[18] But even in the absence of such independents as the Teamsters, such arrangements would not guarantee that rivals would not develop. In the west coast pulp and paper industry in 1964, former AFL and CIO affiliates which had ceased competing for each other's members were challenged by a newly formed independent Association of Western Pulp and Paper Workers, which proceeded to take from them by the election process the right to represent 21,000 of their former constituents.[19] Nevertheless, it is expensive to establish and learn to operate a new union, and our analysis suggests that no-raiding agreements not only eliminate the costs to union treasuries of raiding but also reduce the U^*'s of affiliation with incumbents, thus increasing the range of possible settlements which their leaders can adopt without fear of ouster.

The main objective of the National Labor Relations (Wagner) Act was not, of course, to provide a means of settling representational disputes between unions, but to make it easier for unions to organize workers and for workers, by forming new unions, to organize themselves. N.L.R.B. elections were intended to replace organizational strikes (and the disorder often accompanying them). Such strikes, like elections, can be used to shift from one alternative (no union) to another (a union). The effort required to make the shift is ordinarily much greater, however. The original provisions of the N.L.R.A.—still a fundamental part of federal labor law—reduced the

[16] By a "representational dispute," we mean a dispute between two or more unions over the question of which of them is to act as bargaining agent for a given group of workers. This usage allows us to reserve the term, "jurisdictional dispute," for disputes between two or more unions over the question of whose constituents are to do a given piece of work.

[17] *Constitution of the American Federation of Labor and Congress of Industrial Organizations,* Article xx, "Settlement of Internal Disputes."

[18] American Federation of Labor and Congress of Industrial Organizations, *Proceedings of the Eighth Constitutional Convention;* ... October 2–7, 1969, Washington, AFL-CIO, p. 49.

[19] *Wall Street Journal,* Pacific Coast Edition, Aug. 30, 1965, pp. 1, 10.

effort required to shift from nonunion to union status (and, incidentally, from one union to another). Also, by prohibiting certain retaliatory practices by employers (such as firing workers because of participation in "protected" union activities), the law increased the relative attractiveness of unions.

Especially when shifting of alternatives requires relatively little effort, rival unions will compete to make themselves attractive. At the extreme, competition with a rival union could force the incumbent to the majority wage. Let us return to the situation depicted in Figure 4-2, using the same rules as before: a majority of all workers in Groups *A, B,* and *C* combined will determine who the bargaining representative shall be; the sizes of the groups are such that any two of them constitute a majority. Suppose that there is a rival union which is judged by all three groups to be no more and no less satisfactory than the incumbent on all matters *not* related to the forthcoming wage negotiations. If the incumbent settles for a point other than *M,* its opponent will attack it later, claiming that had it been in charge it would of course have obtained a result which the majority would have preferred to the one they got. Knowing all this, the incumbent union recognizes that *A*'s and *B*'s thresholds move up to their respective indifference curves crossing point *M.* (For *B,* this is $U_2(B)$ in Figure 4-2. *A*'s new threshold is not shown there; it will represent a level of satisfaction superior to $U_2(A)$ and inferior to $U_3(A)$.) In the face of a rival ready to claim that it would have settled at *M,* survival can be had only by obtaining this solution. A lower wage will assure opposition from *B* and *C.* A higher wage may reduce *C*'s U^* (since *C* prefers any wage above *M* to that at *M*) but will lose the votes of *A* and *B.*

Of course, interunion competition is not so perfect that incumbents must usually choose a specific wage rate or go down to defeat. Uncertainty on the parts of unions as well as members, and concerning both the future and the hypothetical past, is one reason for this; its effects are excluded from our formal analysis until a later chapter. Such uncertainty, combined with the passage of time between the signing of a collective agreement and the holding of a representation election, loosens the relationship between the terms of the agreement and the vote at a later date. Also, rivals cannot differentiate their "products" instantly and at will. They come equipped with histories and reputations, and face voters who react to these. While there are many national ("international") unions in the United States which have already paid the costs of establishing themselves and gaining general bargaining and administrative experience, most will not be potential competitors in a given situation. Only a very few will have already acquired experience in the problems of the specific industry, occupation, or class of workers, and these will have an advantage over others. And with or without no-raiding pacts, with one federation or more, collusion plays a role. If X raids part of Y's membership, Y may not honor X's picket lines.

Nonetheless, the presence of actual and potential rival unions may raise U^*'s and narrow the range of alternatives compatible with an incumbent union's survival, and such rivalry may prove beneficial to many of the rank and file. Ralph and Estelle James' *Hoffa and the Teamsters* contains a striking case study of a secessionist movement in the Teamsters' Philadelphia Local 107 in 1963, which caused the union's national leaders to produce a "wage and benefit explosion" for members of the restless local.[20] After considering the fates of other rebellious locals, the authors concluded that "if the Teamsters in a local area want Hoffa to obtain a disproportionately high wage increase for them in the next bargaining session or if they want improved servicing of grievances and job security, they can apparently ensure this by developing a vociferous AFL-CIO minority."[21]

There may be rivalry within a union as well as between unions. We may speak of threshold levels of satisfaction at which a group will not oppose incumbent leaders as well as threshold levels at which it will refrain from supporting a rival union. Either may be higher than the other, depending upon the relative attractiveness and availability of internal and external alternatives to the status quo. The incumbent leadership's preference ordering will then be one in which solutions promising both union survival and reelection are preferred to all others.

If a union is large and its members scattered, its leadership united and its regional officers and press controlled by them, then the process of setting up an opposition slate against the incumbent officers may be very difficult for discontented local officers and rank and filers. Defection to a rival union or to nonunion status may then be the simplest way to revolt. This is especially true in view of the facts that, first, a major cost of forming an opposition within a national union involves interregional communication, and, second, the geographical limits of N.L.R.B. election units are usually small (e.g., one plant or several plants located near one another). In the case of the western

[20]Ralph C. James and Estelle D. James, *Hoffa and the Teamsters: A Study of Union Power* (Princeton: D. Van Nostrand and Company, 1965), pp. 204–209.
[21]*Ibid.*, p. 208.

papermakers mentioned above, no ready-made rival was available. The rebellion was regional and the existing unions national in scope. Forming a rival union was judged easier than taking over existing ones.

But suppose that there already exists an established opposition party with national and regional leaders and access to a press. Suppose that it always enters candidates for national office and that the ballot is secret and truthfully reported. Assume that the election issues will be restricted to the outcome of bargaining with one employer or employer group, and that each party must present the same platform to all voters in a given election. In this case, the incumbents will be forced to the majority wage.

Of course, these assumptions are too limiting. In reality, the incumbents may be given some leeway from past performance of the opposition, from its own handling of internal union administration, and from accusing opponents of nefarious plans or deeds. The leeway may, of course, work on behalf of the opposition. Still, an established opposition will be familiar with the industry. It will often be able to put forward candidates with experience in bargaining and in union administration within the environment in which the members work. Most important of all, the initial investment of establishing an adversary will already have been made. Hence, it seems likely that leaders of a union with an established opposition will be particularly constrained in their choice of bargaining outcomes.

We shall give further consideration to the implications of this analysis for the cohesiveness of two-party unions; but it will be useful to consider first some of the consequences of differences in the boundaries of the "internal" electorate, which votes for the union leadership or for the opposition party, and the "external" electorate, which decides N.L.R.B.-type contests between rival unions. So far we have assumed these electorates to be identical.

Under federal labor law, the National Labor Relations Board has the responsibility of determining the boundaries of the election units within which unions contest with each other and with the alternative of "no union" for the right to represent all the employees in the unit. The employer must bargain with the triumphant union and forswear negotiating with all others respecting the job conditions of the employees in the election unit. (In the law, these are called "bargaining units," but "election units" seems a better term because several of these units are often covered in the same union-employer bargain.) Except for a few statutory provisions (e.g. excluding supervisors from all election units, requiring plant guards and "professional employees" to have separate election units), the Board has wide discretion for deciding electoral boundaries. If an employer has three plants, the Board may decide to establish three one-plant units, or a single unit embracing all three. Often but not inevitably it allows craft or occupational groups within larger aggregations of workers to decide the question of their own destinies in separate elections , often called "Globe elections."[22] Thus, in a steel fabricating plant where most employees are represented by the United Steelworkers of America, a small group of electricians might be granted the right to decide separately whether they wish representation by the Steelworkers, by the International Brotherhood of Electrical Workers, or by no one. Not every group which might wish it can obtain treatment as a separate election unit. In our hypothetical plant, the Board would probably give such a privilege to pattern makers, perhaps to machine fixers, but not to sweepers. And no separate electorate would be accorded to workers over 55, female employees, negroes, Jehovah's Witnesses, or persons who feel union membership to be degrading.

A group which has been granted this option for secession possesses a tool which can be used to influence the policy of the incumbent union on its behalf. There are limits to the extent to which this can be done. The privileged group may not be able to obtain its minimum price for continued affiliation. One limiting factor is the extent of divergence among the preferences of the various groups involved. The second is the availability of alternatives for the other groups, individually and combined. Assume now that an incumbent union wishes to retain the allegiance of the privileged group but, if faced with the choice, would let it go rather than lose its rights to represent the remaining workers who constitute a second election unit. Its preferred solutions will now consist of all those which will secure the adherence of the privileged group *and* of a majority of the remaining workers. This may exclude some solutions which would have been acceptable to the union if there were only one election unit: these are solutions unacceptable to the privileged group but acceptable to a majority of all workers if combined into a single unit.

Let us return to Figure 4-2 and to the situation in which the incumbent union faces the threat of overthrow by another union but is *not* confronted with an internal opposition party. The U_1's are the group thresholds. So long as the three groups formed one election unit, the union preferred solutions on segment FNJ to all others.

---

[22]The policy was initiated in *Globe Machine and Stamping Company,* 3 NLRB 294 (1937).

But now suppose that Group *C* constitutes one election unit and Groups *A* and *B* another. We may imagine that one rival union seeks the right to represent *C*, while another challenges the incumbent for the job of acting as spokesman for *A* and *B* combined. It must also be supposed that on matters other than the forthcoming wage negotiations the rival unions are regarded by electorates *A/B* and *C* as somewhat inferior to the incumbent. Otherwise, our presumption that the U_1's remain thresholds would not make sense. The incumbent union would prefer to continue representing all three groups. If this proved impossible, it would jettison *C* to keep the rest.

Group *C* will be retained by solutions on *GK*. In order to know which solutions will command a majority of votes in the election unit comprising *A* and *B*, we must know which of these is larger. Suppose it is *A*. Then *A/B* will be won by any wage-strike length combination yielding satisfaction to *A* at or above its threshold level of U_1. These outcomes lie on segment *ENH*. Happily for the union, the two segments overlap (*GH*). Hence, points on *GH* are preferred to those on *ENG* (where only *A/B* remains affiliated), which are in turn preferred to all others.

The award of a separate election unit to *C* altered the union's most preferred range of outcomes from *FJ* to *GH*. From *C*'s viewpoint, this change excluded solutions on *FNG* (which it would not have liked at all) and those on *HJ* (which it would have liked very much). But Group *C* is now sure it will obtain an acceptable solution, which was not the case before we made it a separate election unit.

Because it has a majority in the new unit *A/B*, *A* has also gained assurance of at least an acceptable outcome ($U \geq U_1^*(A)$), while losing any hope of a solution close to its own optimum. This result, however, is a special rather than a general one, for it stems from the circumstance that one group holds a majority in the larger of the new election units. This will not always be the case.

Suppose that members of some occupational category *Q* are small minorities in the multioccupational unions which represent them in the various enterprises where they are employed. Suppose further that now, for the first time, members of *Q* are accorded the advantage of separate election units. This change will aid them in two ways. First, of course, majorities can no longer impose upon them unions which they do not want. Second, a potential market for a union (or branch of an existing union) specializing in *Q* has been created, and it is likely that the gap will be filled. As the new union competes with existing ones, *Q*'s U^*'s for the unions now representing them will rise: satisfaction levels—and wage rates—which formerly would have sufficed to secure their allegiance to the older unions will now be rejected. In short, Q's votes count for more and the alternatives are better. The new union may not gain many members, for existing unions may so revise their policies as to keep Q's voters within their ranks. The threat of secession may be enough to gain advantages for Q.

This analysis suggests that Globe-type rules will cause unions to pursue wage structure policies more favorable to the beneficiaries of these rules than would have been followed in their absence. The nearly continuous squeezing of the occupational wage structure in the United States from 1907 to the mid-1950's does not contradict our analysis.[23] For one thing, this tendency can be explained by factors raising the supply of labor equipped with basic skills more rapidly than that of unskilled labor (rising educational levels, cessation of large-scale immigration), and after 1942 by the absence of years with high unemployment (skill differentials increase during bad depressions). Also, unions before the 1930's were confined primarily to those crafts whose members' skills gave them an advantage in organizational strikes. Unionism then operated to maintain skill differentials. The successes of mass-based CIO unions in forcing collective bargaining in such industries as rubber, automobiles, and steel were won at about the time that the Globe policy was promulgated. This was but two years after the passage of the Wagner Act and in the same year that the law was declared constitutional. There has, then, been no period of widespread industrial unionism without opportunities for many craft groups to go, or threaten to go, their separate ways. We suggest an untested conjecture that the N.L.R.B.'s Globe policies may have moderated the decline in skill differentials.

When secession (via election or some other method) is easy for occupational groups within a union, the leadership will be inclined to cater to their wishes, but not to the point of inviting rejection by the rest of their constituents. Hence, if the range of choices compatible with union or leadership survival is narrow, we will expect the union to lose those minorities whose aims diverge substantially from those of the bulk of the membership. The presence of a vigorous rival for the support of the majority can produce this effect, as can competition with an internal opposition for control of the union. A number of American national unions have had two identifiable major factions for short periods of time, but the International Typographical Union is

---

[23] A good summary and evaluation of the evidence may be obtained by combining Everett J. Burtt, Jr., *Labor Markets, Unions, and Government Policies* (New York: St. Martin's Press, 1963), pp. 338–348 with Perlman, *Labor Theory* (New York: Wiley, 1969), pp. 81–104.

unique or nearly so in that it has possessed an institutionalized two-party system (i.e. an established opposition) for decades. It has also witnessed the secession of a series of printing and nonprinting crafts, beginning long before the N.L.R.B. began to hold elections. In their study of the I.T.U., Lipset, Trow, and Coleman concluded that these facets of its history are related, just as our model would predict.[24]

Let us go back once more to our three-group union and simulate the preference ordering of a survival-oriented leadership faced with both external and internal threats. In struggles with rival unions, C is again presumed to form one election unit; a second, in which A holds a majority, consists of A plus B. Internally, there is an opposition party. The groups are assumed to view the two parties as equally acceptable on all matters other than the wage settlement, so that the latter alone will determine whether the incumbent slate of officers will be reelected. These officers will now be forced, as we have seen, to the majority wage. In the situation shown in Figure 4-2, the pressures of internal democracy conflict with the aim of keeping the union intact. Point M is the only one which will secure reelection of the incumbents; but it is unacceptable to Group C, which will secede.

There are aspects of this result which merit further examination. While B will be pleased with the outcome of \$4.80 at M, which is indeed its own optimum, C's departure leaves B at the future mercy of A. A's optimum on this occasion is at \$4.50, below B's. This is unimportant if the differences between B and A or even the existence of the groups are viewed by B as temporary, so that it has no estimate of what preference patterns will look like when the next negotiations occur. In this event, the solution presented above is correct.

But if the divergence of preferences and the relative sizes of the groups are expected to remain about the same, then B cannot be complacent about its future. For the majority wage will move to A's optimum after the departure of Group C. B's preference map has not altered, but its long-term choice lies between G, the minimum for keeping C in the union, and A's optimum of \$4.50 (at point R), which B regards as a portent of A's future preferences. As Figure 4-2 suggests and Figure 4-3 shows more clearly, B will in this particular instance prefer to concede G in order to keep Group C in the union.

Figure 4-3 is a blow-up of that portion of Figure 4-2 which here concerns us. To the original curves we have added, in B's preference

[24]Seymour M. Lipset, Martin A. Trow, and James S. Coleman, *Union Democracy: The Internal Politics of the International Typographical Union* (Glencoe, Ill.: The Free Press, 1956), pp. 298–301.

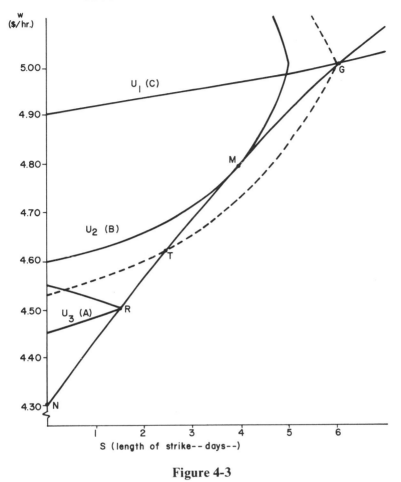

Figure 4-3

map, a new (dashed line) curve slightly to the right of (and thus slightly inferior to) $U_2(B)$. And on the strike length function we have marked an additional point, T. R is A's optimum. B prefers T to R, and is indifferent between T and G. Hence, B prefers G to R. Group A might make a counter-offer of anything between G and T, but acceptance would drive C away and rob B of future protection. Knowing this, B will settle for G. The incumbent leadership will pick G and will be reelected. The union's integrity will be preserved.

Yet, A might be able to seduce B into concurring in C's departure by offering to change the voting rules. If A and B were groups which could be easily defined by external characteristics (e.g. by something other than their preference patterns, such as occupation or location), then an arrangement might be worked out to give *B* a veto with which to dilute *A*'s numerical superiority. For example, each group might elect a wage policy committee, both committees would have to approve any settlement, and *this* arrangement could not be repealed save by majorities of both occupational groups. Such a pact might be visualized as an agreement to split the wage difference between optima in some way. Since there are points which both groups prefer to *G* (i.e. those between *G* and *T*), the arrangement amounts to an offer by *A* to guarantee *B* something always better than *G* (and its future equivalents) as a price for letting *C* go.

In Figure 4-3, such an offer of a future veto would be in effect a promise that future solutions would lie in the equivalent of the segment *GT*. Since *B* prefers these to *G*, it will accept the offer and let *C* leave. Group *A* benefits, because it prefers anything within this range to *G*, the price *B* would have had to pay *C* to keep it in the union.

Finally, still supposing that *B* regards present groupings and preferences as typical of the future, we might redraw the group indifference maps so that *B* regards *R* (*A*'s optimum) as superior to *G*. Then *B* will not seek *C*'s protection, the leadership will pick *M* this time, and *C* will secede. Both *A* and *B* will feel better off with it gone, even though *B* faces a future of submission to *A*. *B*'s behavior, then, rests on its preferences between *A*'s optimum and *C*'s minimum affiliation price, and on whether it regards current groups and preferences as likely to endure.

We conclude that group preference patterns may be such that internal democracy will encourage secession in cases where a leadership without internal opposition would have been able to maintain a united organization. In their study of the I.T.U., Lipset, Trow, and Coleman state:

> . . . a one party system is perhaps necessary for the internal unity and survival of unions whose jurisdiction encompasses many crafts.
>
> Where interest cleavages are inflexible and built into the occupational structure of the union, it would appear that democratic processes not only lead to oppression of the minority subgroup, but that they probably lead to *more* oppression than would rule by one man.[25]

We agree with most of this, but add the contention that a minority

---

[25] *Ibid.*, p. 300.

will ordinarily gain an advantage from one-party rule only if it has a weapon with which the leadership can be threatened. Think of our group C as the "minority subgroup" of the paragraph quoted above. "Democratic processes"—in this context, a two-party system—would force the leadership to the majority wage, M. A secure leadership might move up the strike length function toward G or above it and make C better off. But it might move in the other direction. We can predict that the leadership will move in the direction C prefers only if C possesses an effective means of threatening the leaders.

The opportunity to form a separate union creates one type of threat. Under a one-party regime, it is less likely that the threat will have to be carried out. Refusal to pay dues is another, refusal to honor picket lines a third. In Chapter VII, we shall urge that the possibility that a group will cooperate with others to form an opposition where none exists may also be effective. But without any weapon, a minority can expect to be less oppressed under an entrenched regime only if its interests happen fortuitously to coincide with those of the leaders. For example, a minority might be particularly unwilling to buy higher pay with time on strike; this might agree with the leadership's desire to maintain its treasury, to reduce employer antagonism, or to maintain good relations with government.

We have now analyzed in some detail the formation of union preference orderings in different situations. Before complicating our theory still further, it seems wise to summarize the major characteristics of our basic model, as we have built it up in the last two chapters. A union's leadership must evaluate the several policies which it might pursue with respect to the two bargainable variables, wages and hours. It possesses (by assumption) all relevant information about its members' preferences and the responses of the employer. On this assumption (which we shall abandon in Chapter VI), it is evaluating not only alternative bargaining policies but alternative bargaining outcomes. We find it helpful to portray this evaluation as a preference ordering.

A summary of our basic model as developed to this point follows.

Union Goals

The union's basic goals, which determine its preferences, are presumed to be:

1. survival of the union as collective bargaining representative for at least part of a present or potential constituency; and

2. survival in office of the present union leadership.

Choice between these goals has not presented a problem so far, because whenever there are outcomes satisfying goal (1) and outcomes satisfying goal (2), then there is at least one outcome (the majority wage) satisfying both.

Membership Preferences

Whether a particular wage-hour combination is compatible with union and/or leadership survival depends in part upon membership preference orderings. These, in turn, are determined partially by the values of four nonbargainable variables: the price level, the withholding tax rate, the level of employment of the members, and the length of strike required to obtain the outcome.

It is presumed of membership preference patterns that, other things being equal, the following rules always apply:

1. More real disposable income per worker is preferred to less.
2. More employment is preferred to less.
3. More leisure is preferred to less.
4. Shorter strikes are preferred to longer ones.
5. As a strike lengthens, the increase in wages or leisure necessary to compensate for an extra day's striking rises. (That is, given j, $\delta w/\delta S$ rises along any indifference curve as S increases; given w, $\delta j/\delta S$ rises as S increases.)

In addition, there may (but need not) be one or more target zones of a satisfaction-affecting variable. In the vicinity of these, the willingness to give up other "goods" for more of the variable in question changes sharply.

Finally, the preferences of one group of workers may (but, again, need not) depend upon the real incomes, employment, and leisure experienced by others, and such dependence may extend to the target zones.

Membership Preferences and Union Preferences

Either the survival of a union as collective bargaining agent or the continuance in office of its leadership requires that some groups of constituent workers refrain from opposing it, as they might do by supporting a rival union, failing to participate in a strike, or forming or supporting an internal opposition. To get a group's support, the union must obtain for it at least some minimum level of satisfaction from the bargaining outcome. How high this "threshold" level stands in a group's preference scale depends upon the attractiveness and availability of alternatives.

Constraints on Union Choice

Not all conceivable combinations of the satisfaction-affecting variables are available to the union. Its choice is so contrained that most are unattainable. The constraints are four:

1. The price level is given.
2. Withholding tax rates are given.
3. The employer is free to adjust employment to the wage adopted, and is presumed to do so in a way which will maximize his profit. That is, he will move along the labor demand curve.
4. Some wage-hour combinations are attainable with strikes of some (positive or zero) length. Others are unattainable, either because they are too costly to the employer or because they would leave him with excess demand for labor. (In this sense, the labor supply function constrains union choice, but not in a way likely to be significant.) Furthermore, given the workweek, strike length is a rising function of the wage rate within some range and, within that range, as the wage rate rises the strike time necessary to obtain an extra dollar of wages increases. (That is, along the strike length function, $\delta w/\delta S$ falls as S increases.)

The Context

We have considered several of the contexts within which our general analysis can be applied.

1. Members' preference orderings may be identical or divergent.
2. The threat to union survival may come from a rival union or from the danger of decertification. We have analyzed the relations between membership and union preferences when the choice between rivals will be decided in an N.L.R.B.-type election. The solution depends in part upon the number of election units and their boundaries.
3. A threat to the leadership may arise from an established internal opposition; and this threat may or may not occur in conjunction with threats from outside as described above.
4. We have considered the effect upon the choice among goals compatible with union and/or leadership survival of requirements for membership referenda on wage settlements or dues increases and of leadership commitment to the maximization of net revenue.

Chapter V

THE POLITICO-ECONOMIC MODEL
FORMALIZED

Following the approach developed in the preceding chapters, we shall now set forth a more formal theory of union behavior.[1] Each definition and axiom will be introduced in the text at the point where it is first required. (A complete list of the definitions and axioms used in Chapters V through VII appears as an Appendix.) The familiar wage rate and workweek, price level and employment will be replaced by anonymous x's and k's. This more precise formulation will not only accommodate any number of bargainable and nonbargainable variables but, far more importantly, will enable us in Chapters VI and VII to introduce uncertainty and to explore its implications.

We shall let E stand for the set of all individuals for whom the union seeks to act as bargaining agent. E is partitioned into groups, each composed of one or more individuals. Every individual is a member of one and only one group. G_j denotes the jth group.

Definition i.
$$\mathcal{G} = \{G_1, G_2, \ldots G_j, \ldots G_m\}. \quad G_1 \cup G_2 \cup \cdots \cup G_j \cup \cdots \cup G_m = E,$$
and for all $G_{j'}$, $G_{j''}$, $G_{j'} \cap G_{j''} = \Lambda$, the empty set.

Additional criteria whereby this partition is carried out beyond the requirements stated here are discussed later.

We suppose our union to bargain with the employer about n "bargainable variables," $x_1, x_2, \ldots x_i, \ldots x_n$. The hourly wage rate of sweepers might be x_1, x_2 the hourly wage rate of punch press operators, x_3 the night shift differential, x_4 the method of choosing arbitrators for grievance cases, etc. Any bargainable variable, x_i, can be thought of as a set of all the values x_i', x_i'', etc., which x_i could take. At this stage we must think of all conceivable values and not only of achievable ones. There is a set $\mathcal{X}$ of conceivable bargaining objectives, which is the Cartesian product of all of the bargain-

---

[1]The main elements of the basic logical structure used in developing the models of Chapters V, VI, and VII were used initially in Wallace N. Atherton, "Some Aspects of Trade Union Preferences and Behavior: A Theoretical Analysis," unpublished doctoral dissertation, University of California, Berkeley, 1959.

able variables. That is, $\mathfrak{X}$ comprises all enumerable vectors which include just one value of each bargainable variable.

Definition ii.

$\mathfrak{X} = \{x_1 \times x_2 \times \cdots \times x_i \times \cdots \times x_n\}$ = the set of all $(x_1^i, \ldots x_i^i, \ldots x_n^i)$ such that $x_1^i \in x_1$, and $\ldots$ and $x_i^i \in x_i$ and $\ldots$ and $x_n^i \in x_n$. Thought of as a set of vectors, $\mathfrak{X} = \{X \mid X = (x_1, x_2, \ldots x_i, \ldots x_n)\}$.

- For example, suppose there are two bargainable variables, x_1 and x_2, and that each of them can take two values. Using subscripts to designate the variables and superscripts to stand for the values, we have:

$$x_1 = x_1', x_1''.$$
$$x_2 = x_2', x_2''.$$

And the set $\mathfrak{X}$ —the list of all possible bargaining objectives— consists of:

$$X^{(1)} = x_1', x_2'.$$
$$X^{(2)} = x_1', x_2''.$$
$$X^{(3)} = x_1'', x_2'.$$
$$X^{(4)} = x_1'', x_2''.$$

Our analysis requires the definition of another set of vectors whose components we shall refer to as "nonbargainable variables": $k_1, k_2, \ldots k_i, \ldots k_r$. These are variables which the union cannot influence directly, but which nevertheless affect the satisfaction experienced by its members from any of the possible bargaining outcomes. A common example of such a nonbargainable variable is the consumer price level; another is the quantity of labor demanded by the employer. A variable in K may be a function of one or more variables in X, and in such a case the union may affect the nonbargainable variable indirectly. Thus, the quantity demanded of a particular type of labor will be a function of its wage. But not all k's need be functions of x's, and for the time being we shall not assume any functional relationships between bargainable and nonbargainable variables.

Just as the symbol $\mathfrak{X}$ was introduced to stand for the set of all conceivable bargaining objectives, we shall use $\mathfrak{K}$ to stand for all possible vectors composed of one value of each nonbargainable variable.

Definition iii.
$$\mathfrak{K} = \{k_1 \times k_2 \times \cdots \times k_i \times \cdots \times k_r\} = \text{the set of all } (k_1^i, \ldots k_i^i,$$
$$\ldots k_r^i) \text{ such that } k_1^i \in k_1 \text{ and } \ldots \text{ and } k_i^i \in k_i \text{ and } \ldots \text{ and } k_r^i \in k_r.$$
$$\mathfrak{K} = \{K \mid K = (k_1, k_2, \ldots k_i, \ldots k_r)\}.$$

However, of all the conceivable outcomes in the set $\mathfrak{X}$, there are some which the union can achieve and others which it cannot. The former category, in turn, will often include some which can be attained only by a strike of some length, while other outcomes can be had with no strike at all. The category of outcomes which cannot be achieved consists of those which could not be obtained by a strike of any length. Some of these would be so costly to the employer that he would shut down rather than grant them. Others would be so unattractive to workers that the employer would be left with excess demand for labor.

We now postulate a functional relation between the vectors ("objectives" or "outcomes") and the lengths of strike required to achieve them, S(which may take either positive or zero values). Those objectives which cannot be obtained are outside the domain of this relation. $S(X^{(1)})$, for example, is the length of strike which would be necessary if $X^{(1)}$ were to be obtained. The value of $S(X^{(1)})$ depends entirely upon those factors which determine the employer's behavior. To say that $S(X^{(1)})$ is eleven days means that $X^{(1)}$ can be achieved only by a strike of eleven days. The statement does not imply that the union or its members are willing or unwilling to undertake such a strike.

Axiom i.
$$S = f(X); S \geq 0.$$

On the basis of this strike length function, we now partition the set $\mathfrak{X}$ (all the conceivable outcomes) into two nonintersecting subsets. $\overset{*}{\mathfrak{X}}$ contains only the attainable vectors. The other subset comprises all the outcomes which could not be achieved by a strike of any length.

Definition iv.
$$\overset{*}{\mathfrak{X}} = \{X \mid X \in \mathfrak{X} \text{ and } S = f(X)\}.$$

This treatment of the strike presumes that the employer's willingness to resist is independent of the values taken by the nonbargainable variables in $\mathfrak{K}$. This will not always be the case. For example, the price level will very likely affect the satisfaction experienced by the workers from various wage rates. It is also likely that forces which cause a change in the general price level will affect the demand for the employer's own product and therefore the lengths of time he will hold out before agreeing to various wage rates. $S(X)$, then, may depend on K. If so, the composition of $\overset{*}{\mathfrak{X}}$ will also depend on K. To take this into account, we may write:

Axiom i (a).
   $S = f(X, K); S \geq 0.$

Definition iv (a).

   $\overset{*}{\mathfrak{X}}(K^i) = \{X \mid X \in \mathfrak{X} \text{ and } (K = K^i) \rightarrow S = f(X)\}.$

We shall now specify group preference orderings over alternative situations $[X, S(X), K]$. Each situation consists of one value of each x (bargainable variable), one value of each k (nonbargainable variable), and the strike length implied. These preference orderings are assumed to be transitive. The i'th situation may be written $[X, S(X), K]^i$ or $[X, K]^i$, explicit reference to S being unnecessary because it is a function of X. $[X, K]^{(1)} >_j [X, K]^{(2)}$ and $[X, K]^{(2)} \sim_m [X, K]^{(3)}$ mean, respectively, that the j'th group prefers situation $[X,K]^{(1)}$ to $[X,K]^{(2)}$ while the m'th group is indifferent between $[X,K]^{(2)}$ and $[X,K]^{(3)}$.

We shall let T stand for the union, to which each group may or may not be affiliated. For each group, every value of (X, K) implies either affiliation or nonaffiliation with T; indifference about affiliation is not allowed. Furthermore, any (X, K) implying affiliation is preferred to any (X, K) implying nonaffiliation. Unattainable outcomes always imply nonaffiliation.

Axiom ii.
   For all G_j, either $G_j \in T$ or $G_j \notin T$.

Axiom iii.
   For all G_j, $\{(X, K)^{(1)} \rightarrow (G_j \in T) \text{ and } (X, K)^{(2)} \rightarrow (G_j \notin T)\} \rightarrow \{(X, K)^{(1)} >_j (X, K)^{(2)}\}.$

Axiom iv.
   For all G_j, $\{(X, K)^{(1)} \rightarrow (G_j \in T) \text{ and } (X, K)^{(1)} \sim (X, K)^{(2)}\} \rightarrow \{(X, K)^{(2)} \rightarrow (G_j \in T)\}.$

Axiom v.
   For all G_j, $X \notin \overset{*}{\mathfrak{X}} \rightarrow G_j \notin T$.

It should be noted that the implications run in only one direction in these axioms.

We shall refer to those (X, K) implying $G_j \in T$ as (G_j)'s "affiliation set," and to (X, K)'s implying $G_j \notin T$ as G_j's "nonaffiliation set." Either (but not both) of these sets may be empty.

Now that the group preference orderings have been introduced, we can say more about the basis of the partition of E into groups in Definition *i* above. There, we specified only that no two groups intersect and that the union of all groups be coextensive with E. Underlying our conception of a group is the requirement that no two groups may have identical preference orderings. If $G_{j'}$ and $G_{j''}$ are two groups, then at least one of three things must be true. Either there is some pair of alternatives $(X, K)^{(1)}$ and $(X, K)^{(2)}$ such that $G_{j'}$ prefers $(X, K)^{(1)}$ while $G_{j''}$ prefers $(X, K)^{(2)}$, or one group is indifferent between such a pair while the other is not, or there is some alternative which is in $(G_{j'})$'s affiliation set but in $(G_{j''})$'s non-affiliation set. If none of these three conditions obtains, then $G_{j'}$ and $G_{j''}$ are the same group.

The logical structure of the arguments to follow does not require the introduction of individuals' preference orderings; in order, however, to "pin down" the idea of a union composed of internally homogeneous groups partly at odds with each other, we may think of individuals as being the elements of E, which is partitioned into groups. Every element can be found in one and only one group. The preference ordering of any element will be identical to that of the group in which it is found, and the individual's affiliation and dis-affiliation sets are also those of his group. If two individuals have preference orderings which differ with respect to any pair of alternatives, then they must be in different groups.

An almost identical concept of "group" was used in Chapter IV, so that the reader may by now be accustomed to it. But because the use to which we put this term has confused some readers and hearers of preliminary drafts of parts of this work, it seems wise to discuss it further.

Corresponding to the concepts employed in building our model are the real-world phenomena which inspired them. In the act of abstraction, only some of the observed characteristics of the real phenomena are attributed to their counterparts in the model. Others are omitted. Without many such omissions, theories would seldom if ever be built.

A real-world phenomenon corresponding to our E would be a collection of employees of a single employer, or employees of several employers related by being in the same product market, labor market, or employers' association. A real-world phenomenon corresponding to *T* would be a trade union representing or seeking to represent the people in *E* and faced by the problem of choosing to pursue one of a set of bargaining objectives or policies rather than others. At least some of the employees in the real-world prototype of *E* would have preferences concerning which bargaining objectives they thought the union should pursue. After talking with some of them, we might find that most people in certain identifiable groups had preferences about bargaining objectives typical of their own groups but not of others. For example, well-paid high seniority tool-makers might favor equal percentage increases for all employees and be uninterested in expanding bumping rights. ("*A* bumps *B*" means that *A*, his former job having been temporarily or permanently eliminated, takes *B*'s job away from him. When layoffs occur, many collective agreements permit higher seniority employees to bump lower seniority employees within whatever departmental, skill, or other constraints may be specified in the agreement.) On the other hand, semiskilled production workers with medium seniority might advocate equal absolute increases for all employees and favor strongly an expansion of bumping ranges. We would then say that these and other groups—which we might identify in terms of sex, age, seniority, current pay rate, skill, and other characteristics— have different preferences about the bargaining policies which their union might pursue. For its part, the union has the job of somehow resolving these differences into a preference pattern of its own and picking as its objective a "package" which most or all of the employees will endorse and strike for if necessary. Indeed, attainment of this objective should, from the viewpoint of the union's leaders, leave most or all employees staunch unionists, willing to vote for a dues increase and quite deaf to the blandishments of rival unions, of minority factions seeking to oust the union's incumbent leadership, or of company newsletters insinuating that management is the worker's best friend and union dues a financial burden yielding little return.

In our *model, E* is defined as a set of individuals, but these individuals are partitioned into *m* groups called $G_1, \ldots G_j, \ldots G_m$, and in nearly all of the analysis *E* is treated as consisting of these groups. In the model, the group are *not* defined in terms of pay, seniority, sex, skill, department, job, race, religion, etc. They *are* defined in just two ways. One is in terms of their preference orderings. There are at least as many groups as there are preference orderings actually held by one or more individuals. At one extreme, suppose that every individual in *E* had a preference ordering differing from that of every other individual in E. Then, each individual would constitute a separate group. At the other extreme, suppose that everyone in E had the same preference ordering. Then there might be just one group. Groups may be distinguished by one other attribute in the model. This has to do with the circumstances under which they are affiliated or not affiliated with the union. ("Affiliation" will take on different specific meanings in different versions of our model later on; for the time being, "affiliation with" can be thought of as synonymous with "membership in.") A group affiliates with, remains affiliated or unaffiliated with, or ceases affiliation with the union *in toto*. For some preferred bargaining objectives, a group will be in the union; for others it will be out. As possible limiting cases, a group might be affiliated with the union in the cases of all objectives or in the cases of none.

If, then, G_1 and G_2 are two different groups, it must be that:

1. their preference orderings are not identical, and/or
2. their affiliation sets differ.

The assumption that a group is internally homogeneous explains why we assume its preferences to be transitive. The reader who accepts this assumption as applied to individuals in other contexts (such as demand theory) cannot object to supposing it of our groups. (Indeed, the real-world counterpart of the buying unit in demand theory is usually a household composed of several persons, so that our abstraction from intragroup differences in preferences is not so novel as it may seem.)

So far, we have been engaged in compiling a list of properties attributed to a "model" union whose behavior we seek to analyze. These are: the partitioning of a collection of actual or potential members of the union into groups with divergent (i.e. nonidentical) preferences with respect to bargaining objectives, strikes, and the nonbargainable variables; the postulating of lists of bargainable and nonbargainable variables and strike lengths upon which the preference orderings of these groups depend; the introduction of group affiliation and nonaffiliation sets; and the assumption that length of strike necessary to obtain a given bargaining objective varies with the objective sought. This list of properties is one necessary step toward our goal, which is the analysis of the behavior under various specified circumstances of a union characterized by internal heterogeneity. In addition to this description, our analysis requires some assumptions about the state of knowledge of the union's leadership (by which we mean those who formulate its policy) concerning the nature of some of the relations contained in the list above.

We shall suppose our leadership to have correct and complete knowledge of the preference orderings over X, $S(X)$, K of its constituent groups, and to know which values of $(X, S(X), K)$ fall into the affiliation set of each group. For the time being, we shall also presume perfect knowledge on the part of the leadership of the strike length function, $S(X)$, and perfect foresight about levels of the variables in K. Certainty about $S(X)$ and K will be eliminated at a later stage.

We must now develop one or more hypotheses which suggest how a union leadership could have a preference ordering among alternative objectives which it might pursue in the face of divergent preference orderings among the membership. In focusing on this aspect of policy making, we do not mean to suggest that internal differences are the only pressures upon union leadership. Behind the $S(X)$ function lie many market forces which are transmitted by the employer. It suffices for our purposes to suppose that a certain group of possible outcomes falls in the attainable set and that the $S(X)$ distribution assumes some shape. Were we to explain the partition and the shape, we would need to analyze the impact of product and factor market conditions and their consequences, giving consideration to such things as the price and income elasticities of demand for the employer's product, his expected pattern of sales during the contract period, the degree of unionization of the industry, the possibilities of substitution between labor and other factors, etc.

As we did in Chapter IV, we shall begin by adopting what may be called a "survival approach" in theorizing about union policy formation. This approach starts with the question, "With what preference ordering would the probability of union survival be greatest?" To give meaningful answers to this question, the conditions of union survival must be meaningfully stated. The resulting preference ordering will depend on the nature of the threat with which the union is faced.

The first type of threat to union survival for which we shall formulate a hypothesis and infer a preference ordering was introduced in Chapter IV. It is suggested by the election procedure used by the National Labor Relations Board and some state labor relations agencies: the union, to obtain or to keep exclusive bargaining rights, must receive in an election a majority of the votes cast by the workers for whom it is, or seeks to become, the certified bargaining representative. As formulated, this hypothesis assumes that the union must obtain a majority of all eligible voters, while the N.L.R.B. requires only a majority of participating voters. However, the percentage of eligibles who cast valid ballots in N.L.R.B. elections is usually quite large—88.9% in the five fiscal years from 1965–66 through 1969–70—so that the discrepancy seems unimportant.[2] Also, as in Chapter IV, we are assuming only two alternatives on the ballot, whereas there might be several. Introduction of a third alternative into an otherwise unchanged situation may change the union's preference ordering.

In the context of this kind of survival threat the idea of a group's affiliation with the union takes on particular significance. "$G_j \in T$" means that, in a representation election, the members of G_j will vote in favor of the designation or retention of T as their bargaining agent. Axioms iii and iv state that all bargaining objectives in a group's affiliation set are preferred to all objectives in its nonaffiliation set. Here, this means that the achievement of an objective low enough in a group's preference ordering to be in its nonaffiliation set will lead to that group's voting against the union in the election. Thus, the group's vote for or against the union is made to depend upon the bargaining objective achieved, the length of strike necessary to obtain it, and the vector of nonbargainable variables.

Definition v.

Let n_j be the number of individuals in G_j and let $N = \sum_{j=1}^{m} n_j$, which is the number of individuals for whom the union has or seeks representational rights. $G_{j'} \in T \rightarrow n_{j'} \in T$. To every $(X, K)^i$ there corresponds some $\sum_{j=1}^{m} n_j \mid n_j \in T$.

The condition, $\sum_{j=1}^{m} n_j \mid n_j \in T > N/2$, is the union's survival condition. Since the union prefers survival to nonsurvival, objectives implying this condition will be preferred to those which do not. Under our temporary assumptions of perfect knowledge and foresight the value of K is fixed and foreseen. To every X there corresponds one value of $S(X)$. In describing alternative situations, then, we can write X^i rather than $[X, S(X), K]^i$, so long as we keep in mind that any preference ordering over X takes $S(X)$ into account and might be altered were a change in either $S(X)$ or K to occur.

[2] United States National Labor Relations Board, *Annual Reports of the National Labor Relations Board,* Thirty-First through Thirty-Fifth, for Fiscal Years Ending June 30, 1966 through June 30, 1970 (Washington: United States Government Printing Office), Tables 13 and 14.

Since K is known, our formulation of the union's preferences will be valid whether or not some of the k's are functionally related to some of the x's and whether or not S is a function of both X and K rather than of X alone. Using the subscript, u, to indicate the union's preference ordering,

$$\text{I.} \left\{ X^{(1)} \rightarrow \sum_{j=1}^{m} n_j \mid n_j \in T > \frac{N}{2} \right.$$

and

$$\left. X^{(2)} \rightarrow \sum_{j=1}^{m} n_j \mid n_j \in T \leq \frac{N}{2} \right\} \leftrightarrow X^{(1)} >_u X^{(2)}.$$

$$\text{II.} \left\{ X^{(1)} \rightarrow \sum_{j=1}^{m} n_j \mid n_j \in T > \frac{N}{2} \right.$$

and

$$\left. X^{(2)} \rightarrow \sum_{j=1}^{m} n_j \mid n_j \in T > \frac{N}{2} \right\}$$

or

$$\left\{ X^{(1)} \rightarrow \sum_{j=1}^{m} n_j \mid n_j \in T \leq \frac{N}{2} \right.$$

and

$$\left. X^{(2)} \rightarrow \sum_{j=1}^{m} n_j \mid n_j \in T \leq \frac{N}{2} \right\} \leftrightarrow X^{(1)} \sim_u X^{(2)}.$$

We have, then, a union preference ordering, although not a very elaborate one. There are just two classes of objectives: preferred ones, which lead to survival, and nonpreferred ones, which will put the union out of business. Uncertainty about strike lengths and about future values of K will make the matter more complex, but before introducing these complications we shall illustrate the model under conditions of certainty about K and L by means of a hypothetical example.

Suppose that E consists of three groups, and that $n_1 = 40$, $n_2 = 30$, and $n_3 = 30$. $N/2$, then, is 50. Suppose also that there are three bargainable variables which can take two values each. $\mathfrak{X}$, then, consists of:

$$X^{(1)} = x_1', x_2', x_3'. \qquad X^{(5)} = x_1'', x_2', x_3'.$$

$$X^{(2)} = x_1', x_2', x_3''. \qquad X^{(6)} = x_1'', x_2', x_3''.$$

$$X^{(3)} = x_1', x_2'', x_3'. \qquad X^{(7)} = x_1'', x_2'', x_3'.$$

$$X^{(4)} = x_1', x_2'', x_3''. \qquad X^{(8)} = x_1'', x_2'', x_3''.$$

$X^{(1)}$, however, is unattainable, so that $\overset{*}{\mathfrak{X}} = \{X^{(2)}, X^{(3)}, X^{(4)}, X^{(5)}, X^{(6)}, X^{(7)}, X^{(8)}\}$.

The strike length function is:

X	$S(X)$ in weeks
$X^{(2)}$	5
$X^{(3)}$	4
$X^{(4)}$	4
$X^{(5)}$	3
$X^{(6)}$	2
$X^{(7)}$	1
$X^{(8)}$	0

Since K is known, all we need say about it is that changes in its value might affect any group's preference ordering over the X's and/or the partition of X into affiliation and nonaffiliation sets for each group. But given the foreknown value of K, we presume the preference orderings of the three groups over the obtainable objectives and their affiliation sets to be (R stands for rank):

R	$G_1(n_1 = 40)$		$G_2(n_2 = 30)$		$G_3(n_3 = 30)$	
1	$X^{(2)} G_1 \in T$		$X^{(6)} G_2 \in T$		$X^{(5)} G_3 \in T$	
2	$X^{(3)}$	''	$X^{(2)}$	''	$X^{(7)}$	''
3	$X^{(4)}$	''	$X^{(7)}$	''	$X^{(6)}$	''
4	$X^{(5)}$	''	$X^{(5)}$	''	$X^{(2)}$	''
5	$X^{(7)} G_1 \notin T$		$X^{(8)}$	''	$X^{(3)}$	''
6	$X^{(6)}$	''	$X^{(3)} G_2 \notin T$		$X^{(8)} G_3 \notin T$	
7	$X^{(8)}$	''	$X^{(4)}$	''	$X^{(4)}$	''

The implications with respect to affiliation and votes, then, are:

X	$G_j \mid G_j \in T$	$\sum n_j \mid n_j \in T$
$X^{(1)}$	none; unattainable	—
$X^{(2)}$	G_1, G_2, G_3	100
$X^{(3)}$	G_1, G_3	70

$X^{(4)}$	G_1	40
$X^{(5)}$	G_1, G_2, G_3	100
$X^{(6)}$	G_2, G_3	60
$X^{(7)}$	G_2, G_3	60
$X^{(8)}$	G_2	30

According to our rule, outcomes which yield more than 50 votes for the union will be preferred to those which do not. So, the union's preference ordering is:

$$X^{(2)} \sim X^{(3)} \sim X^{(5)} \sim X^{(6)} \sim X^{(7)} > X^{(4)} \sim X^{(8)}.$$

Note that according to our criterion the union is indifferent between objective $X^{(2)}$ and objective $X^{(3)}$, even though the former will yield it a unanimous affirmative vote and the latter a majority of only 70 to 30. Either outcome, however, will lead to the union's certification as bargaining agent.

A different criterion would allow our union to prefer larger majorities to smaller ones, still preferring any majority to any defeat. Using $\sum n_j(X)^i$ to mean the $\sum_{j=1}^m n_j \mid n_j \in T$ implied by X^i, and letting $X^{(1)}$ and $X^{(2)}$ stand for *any* pair of possible objectives:

I. $\left\{ \sum n_j(X^{(1)}) > \dfrac{N}{2} \right.$

and

$$\left. \sum n_j(X^{(2)}) > \dfrac{N}{2} \right\} \rightarrow \{[\sum n_j(X^{(1)}) > \sum n_j(X^{(2)}) \rightarrow X^{(1)} >_u X^{(2)}]$$

and

$$[\sum n_j(X^{(1)}) = \sum n_j(X^{(2)}) \rightarrow X^{(1)} \sim_u X^{(2)}]\}.$$

II. $\left\{ \sum n_j(X^{(1)}) > \dfrac{N}{2} \right.$

and

$$\left. \sum n_j(X^{(2)}) \mid \le \dfrac{N}{2} \right\} \rightarrow \{X^{(1)} >_u X^{(2)}\}.$$

III. $\left\{ \sum n_j(X^{(1)}) \le \dfrac{N}{2} \right.$

and

$$\left. \sum n_j(X^{(2)}) \leq \frac{N}{2} \right\} \rightarrow \{X^{(1)} \sim_u X^{(2)}\}.$$

One might argue for such a criterion on the grounds mentioned earlier that the larger its majority, the more will the union be able to impress the employer, the nonunion minority, and any rival unions with the appearance of permanence.

The maximization of net revenues rather than of votes provides an alternative criterion for choice by the union leadership among outcomes which are equally acceptable from the viewpoint of institutional survival. The general principles of our analysis in Chapter IV still hold. That is, gross revenues rise with the number of dues paying members, while costs are directly related to the length of the strike. If all outcomes include a union shop, the leadership will prefer that one (or those) of the objectives promising institutional survival which is (are) associated with the smallest strike to all others.[3] (In our most recent example, this would be $X^{(7)}$.) If there is no possibility of a union shop, the net revenues associated with each X will vary directly with the proportion of workers willing to pay dues, directly with employment and hence inversely with each of the negotiated wage rates, and inversely with the length of strike. And in our new formulation of the problem, the union security clause may itself be one of the bargainable variables. As this provision is stronger or weaker, the proportion of members who will pay dues *given* the values of the rest of the x's becomes larger or smaller.

Finally, we shall consider the effects of a requirement that no agreement may become operative unless ratified by a majority vote of the membership. Once again, the effects of such a rule will accord with the objective of institutional survival, but not always with the retention of minorities who constitute separate electorates in N.L.R.B.-type certification polls. And, again, such a rule may force a net revenue-oriented leadership into a longer strike than it would wish to undertake. While these conclusions remain valid, the expan-

---

[3] This conclusion requires the seemingly reasonable assumption that outcomes which require long strikes do not generate enough additional employment to offset, via greater dues income, the costs of striking. In the model used in Chapter IV, strike length and employment were inversely related through the wage rate. Hence, under union shop conditions, strike length and net revenues were also inversely related. Our present model, however, contains no explicit assumption that X's requiring longer strikes will bring less employment.

sion of our model to include any number of bargainable variables creates complications which were absent in our earlier investigation. These have to do with the possibility of intransitivity in majority voting. More precisely, this difficulty arises because we have eliminated certain restrictive assumptions (such as "higher wages are preferred to lower ones") about our group preference orderings; in a model with many bargainable variables, making equally stringent assumptions about all of them seems unwise.

The example of a three-group union introduced above will be used to illustrate the effects of a majority ratification requirement. As before, $n_1 = 40$, $n_2 = 30$, $n_3 = 30$, and the group preference orderings and affiliation sets are presumed to be:

Rank	G_1	G_2	G_3
1	$X^{(2)}$	$X^{(6)}$	$X^{(5)}$
2	$X^{(3)}$	$X^{(2)}$	$X^{(7)}$
3	$X^{(4)}$	$X^{(7)}$	$X^{(6)}$
4	$X^{(5)}$	$X^{(5)}$	$X^{(2)}$
5	$X^{(7)}$	$X^{(8)}$	$X^{(3)}$
6	$X^{(6)}$	$X^{(3)}$	$X^{(8)}$
7	$X^{(8)}$	$X^{(4)}$	$X^{(4)}$

The horizontal lines divide each group's affiliation and nonaffiliation sets. The number of votes for the union as bargaining agent (inferred from the table above) and the strike length (which must be assumed) associated with each X are, as before:

X	$\sum n_j \mid n_j \in T$	$S(X)$
$X^{(1)}$	—	unattainable
$X^{(2)}$	100	5
$X^{(3)}$	70	4
$X^{(4)}$	40	4
$X^{(5)}$	100	3
$X^{(6)}$	60	2
$X^{(7)}$	60	1
$X^{(8)}$	30	0

From a survival viewpoint, the outcomes acceptable to the union are: $X^{(2)}$, $X^{(3)}$, $X^{(5)}$, $X^{(6)}$, and $X^{(7)}$. If a union shop were included in all attainable outcomes and if the union's leaders wished to maximize net revenue, their optimum would be $X^{(7)}$. But now suppose that no solution is binding unless approved by a majority of the membership.

Let us imagine what would happen if the membership voted on all possible pairs of objectives ($X^{(2)}$ vs. $X^{(3)}$; $X^{(2)}$ vs. $X^{(4)}$, etc.). We do not expect actual union meetings to do this, but the hypothetical experiment is useful nonetheless. Its result would be a rank ordering, decided by majority vote, over the objectives. Such an ordering may be entirely transitive or it may be partially or wholly intransitive. Intransitivity in the majority rank ordering is perfectly compatible with the transitive preferences which we continue to assume for each group; where it occurs, it is the product of shifts in the composition of the majority.[4]

Our example has been so constructed as to provide an instance of such intransitivity. One majority (G_1 and G_2) prefers $X^{(2)}$ to $X^{(5)}$; another (G_1 and G_3) prefers $X^{(5)}$ to $X^{(6)}$, and, completing the circle, a third majority (G_2 and G_3) favors $X^{(6)}$ over $X^{(2)}$. Furthermore, groups G_1 and G_3 prefer $X^{(5)}$ to $X^{(7)}$ and $X^{(7)}$ to $X^{(6)}$; but G_1 and G_2 constitute a majority preferring $X^{(2)}$ to $X^{(7)}$. Thus, we have four alternatives ($X^{(2)}, X^{(5)}, X^{(6)}$, and $X^{(7)}$) involved in majority-intransitive relations with one another. But each of these four alternatives is preferred by some majority to each other possible outcome (i.e. to $X^{(3)}$ and to $X^{(4)}$ and to $X^{(8)}$). Let us refer to the four preferred objectives as the set $[X_m]$. Below $[X_m]$ the majority rank ordering (using the subscript m to stand for "majority") is $[X_m] >_m X^{(3)} >_m X^{(8)} >_m X^{(4)}$, and is conveniently transitive. But within $[X_m]$, we have:

$$X^{(2)} >_m X^{(5)}. \qquad X^{(2)} >_m X^{(7)}.$$
$$X^{(5)} >_m X^{(6)}. \qquad X^{(5)} >_m X^{(7)}.$$
$$X^{(6)} >_m X^{(2)}.$$
$$X^{(7)} >_m X^{(6)}.$$

Corresponding to the majority wage of Chapter IV, we define a "majority objective," X_m. This is a value of the vector X such that there is no other single value of X which a majority would prefer to it. But while there was always a unique majority wage in our earlier analysis, now there may or may not be a unique majority objective. There will, however, always be a majority set of possible objectives,

[4] The outstanding modern work on this range of problems is Kenneth J. Arrow, *Social Choice and Individual Values* (Cowles Foundation Monograph 12, New York: John Wiley and Sons, 1951 and 1963).

$[X_m]$. There is no value of X outside of this set which a majority would prefer to *any* value within it. At one extreme, $[X_m]$ may include all attainable outcomes. At the other, it includes just one: the unique majority objective. Except for the latter case, and ignoring the possibility of tied votes (the majority-rule analog of indifference in individual orderings), each objective within $[X_m]$ is ranked higher than at least one of the other members of the set, and each objective within $[X_m]$ is ranked below at least one other member. In our example, $[X_m]$ is composed of $X^{(2)}$, $X^{(5)}$, $X^{(6)}$, and $X^{(7)}$.

If there is a majority set and if the membership is allowed to vote as it would in a continuous membership meeting, outcomes outside of the set will be rejected. If all alternatives were considered simultaneously, there would be no solution: one pictures a meeting which votes to substitute motions for each other in an endless chain, never reaching a decision. (For example, in our example, $X^{(5)}$ is moved, $X^{(2)}$ is substituted, $X^{(6)}$ replaces $X^{(2)}$, $X^{(7)}$ supersedes $X^{(6)}$, we go back to $X^{(5)}$ again, and so on.) But we are saved from this result by presuming that alternatives come before the membership in a sequence imposed by the strike length function. What happens depends upon what the groups know about each others' preference orderings. Two suppositions about this knowledge yield different results.

First, each group may know nothing of the desires of the others. It will vote against possible settlements until the proposal being discussed is superior in its own preference ordering to all which might be won by striking further. The strike will continue until groups constituting a majority find themselves in this position. In our example, all alternatives will be rejected until $X^{(2)}$ is obtained after five weeks. $X^{(6)}$—which a majority would have preferred to $X^{(2)}$—will have been turned down because, when it was proposed after the second week, both G_1 and G_3 voted against it. G_1 preferred any future outcome to $X^{(6)}$. G_3 (for which $X^{(5)} > X^{(6)} > X^{(2)}$), could still hope for $X^{(5)}$. When $X^{(5)}$ came up after the third week, however, G_1 and G_2 would have combined to reject it and press on to $X^{(2)}$. If the reader will rearrange $S(X)$ for the X's in the majority set, leaving the group preference orderings the same, he can cause our model union to adopt any of the outcomes in $[X_m]$.

Alternatively, we may presume that the groups know each others' preferences as well as their own. Rational voting which takes such knowledge into account may alter the results. This would be the case in our example, in which mutual awareness of preferences leads to the adoption of $X^{(7)}$ rather than $X^{(2)}$. The elements in the majority set would—if the strike lasted long enough—be brought to the membership for ratification or rejection in the order $X^{(7)}$, $X^{(6)}$, $X^{(5)}$, $X^{(2)}$. Consider what happens when, after one week of strike, settlement $X^{(7)}$ is proposed. This is not any group's optimum. If the strike were to last through the third week when $X^{(5)}$ would become available, a majority would vote to press further since $X^{(2)}$—after five weeks—is ranked above $X^{(5)}$. But $X^{(6)} >_m X^{(2)}$. So, after two weeks, $X^{(6)}$ would be adopted in order to avoid $X^{(2)}$. The real choice, then, lies between $X^{(6)}$ and $X^{(7)}$. Both G_1 and G_3 prefer $X^{(7)}$; only G_2 prefers $X^{(6)}$. Hence $X^{(7)}$ will be ratified. (G_1 will be so disgruntled that it will vote against the union in a bargaining election, but it votes for $X^{(7)}$ because the alternative of $X^{(6)}$ is from its viewpoint even worse.)

One result of our analysis is that if the leadership is interested (as for revenue purposes) in settling for the shortest strike consistent with survival, it may be to its advantage to encourage the dissemination among the groups of correct information about each others' preferences. Generally, however, our exploration of the implications of intransitive majority rankings does not alter the main results of our earlier discussion of membership voting. If all possible solutions are put before the membership as they arise, the leadership will be forced to a solution in the majority set. The outcome may, as before, be influenced by so controlling the frequency of meetings as to exclude from consideration some alternatives in $[X_m]$ which are relatively unpalatable to the leadership.

CHAPTER VI

UNCERTAINTY INTRODUCED

We shall now introduce some elements of uncertainty into the model set forth in Chapter V. We shall continue to suppose that our union leadership knows precisely the preference orderings and affiliation sets of the groups. Uncertainty enters in that we shall now suppose neither perfect foresight about levels of the variables in K nor perfect knowledge of the strike length function, $S(X)$, on the leadership's part. But while it lacks certainty, the leadership is not without ideas about future levels of the nonbargainable variables, and regards some values as more likely than others. It can be thought of, then, as acting as if, for each k, it attached a probability to every possible value. These probabilities are subjective probabilities in the sense that they are based upon the leadership's estimate of the significance of the (ordinarily incomplete) information available to it. We suppose that for each k_i there is a function $P_i = P_i(k_i)$; $0 \le P \le 1$.

Similarly, while the union does not have perfect foresight regarding the strike length necessary to obtain each objective, it does, for each objective, regard some strike lengths as more likely than others. While there would in fact be some unique $S(X)$ corresponding to every X, the union could not be certain of any one of these magnitudes until the strike (if any) was over and the contract signed. From the point of view of the union leadership about to formulate bargaining objectives, we shall think of $S(X)$ as a relationship in which a distribution of the probabilities of all values of $S(X)$ varies as X varies. There are two ways of looking at this relationship, and we shall need both of them. First, to *each* X^i there corresponds a probability distribution $P_i = P_i[S(X^i)]$; $0 \le P \le 1$. That is, for a specific outcome—say $X^{(5)}$—there is some probability that it can be obtained without any strike ($S = 0$), some other probability that it can be achieved with a strike of one week ($S = 1$), some probability that it will require a strike of two weeks, and so on. Our second approach to the same distribution involves looking at a given strike length (such as two weeks), rather than at a given outcome. There is some probability that seeking outcome $X^{(1)}$ will lead to a strike of two weeks, some probability that seeking outcome $X^{(2)}$ will involve a strike of two weeks, etc. Thus, $P(S = 0)$ is a function of X; so are $P(S = 1)$, $P(S = 2)$, etc. These probabilities, like those attached to the k's, are dependent upon the leadership's estimates of the situation, based on the information available to it.

As was suggested in the previous chapter, the values taken by some of the k's may affect the strike length function—as when a rise in aggregate demand increases the price level (one of the k's) and simultaneously reduces employer resistance to wage pressure. In this case, the shape of each $P_i [S(X^i)]$ depends on K, and we are dealing with conditional probabilities. Then, for example, $P_5[S(X^{(5)}) = 1] =$ $P(K^{(1)}) \cdot P_{K^{(1)}} [S(X^{(5)}) = 1] + P(K^{(2)}) \cdot P_{K^{(2)}} [S(X^{(5)}) = 1] + \ldots.$ That is, the probability that $X^{(5)}$ can be had with a strike of just one week is equal to the probability that K will equal $K^{(1)}$ times the probability that in this event $X^{(5)}$ can be won after a week, plus the probability that $K = K^{(2)}$ times the probability that in that event $X^{(5)}$ can be won after a week, and so on through all the possible values of K. It should be noted that, while we introduce uncertainty about K and S, we continue to presume leadership omniscience concerning group preference orderings. We believe that uncertainty about K and S adds to the value of our model but that adding still more probability distributions would increase the difficulty of describing our conclusions without any offsetting gains. Furthermore, information about constituents' attitudes toward possible changes in X and K as well as evidence of their willingness to strike is accessible to the leaders, and, indeed, when issues of concern to the members are involved, may be pressed upon the officials quite vigorously. On the other hand, estimates of the strike length function and of the variables in K involve predictions of future events which are mainly beyond the union's influence. And, in the case of $S(X)$, the employer may have an interest in maintaining secrecy.

Before proceeding further, it should be noted that the probabilistic elements in this theory are due solely to the absence of perfect foresight, that we make no assumptions about the shapes of the distributions of $P(k_i)$ and $P(S)$ and that we make no attempt to explain whatever shapes the distributions take. That is, we do not theorize about the way in which particular past and present events cause a union's leadership to act as if the probability distribution of a particular nonbargainable variable has a particular shape.

We have postulated probability distributions $P_1(k_1)$, $P_2(k_2)$, etc. From these can be constructed a distribution of probabilities of the vectors in $\mathcal{K}$. Using k'_1 to stand for the value taken by variable k_1 in vector K', we know from Definition iii that

$$K' = (k'_1, k'_2, k'_3, \ldots),$$

$$K'' = (k_1'', k_2'', k_3'', \ldots), \text{ etc.}$$

Each vector differs from every other vector with respect to the magnitude of at least one of its elements. k_2' is the fixed value taken by the variable k_2 in the vector K', and it may or may not be equal in magnitude to k_2'' in K'', for example. The magnitude of at least one element (k_i) in K' must differ from its magnitude in K''.

The probability of any particular vector in $\mathcal{K}$, then, if its elements are independent, is the product of the probabilities of all its elements. Thus,

$$P(K') = P(k_1') \cdot P(k_2') \cdot \ldots \cdot P(k_r');$$
$$P(K'') = P(k_1'') \cdot P(k_2'') \cdot \ldots \cdot P(k_r'').$$

If the k's are correlated with one another, then $P(K') = P(k_1') \cdot P_{k_1'}(k_2') \cdot P_{k_1', k_2'}(k_3') \cdot \ldots P_{k_1', \ldots k_{r-1}'}(k_r')$.

There is also the possibility that some of the $P_i(k_i)$'s depend upon the value of X. For example, employment—which is not bargainable directly in the ordinary case and is therefore one of the k's—may depend on wage rates. If the value of a nonbargainable variable which affects group preference orderings is completely determined by the values of one or more bargainable variables, then the former need not be included in K at all; the preference orderings will reflect its impact. But a nonbargainable variable may depend only partly upon one or more bargainable variables and partly upon other things, and in this event the probability distribution assumed by the nonbargainable variable will vary depending upon the values of the relevant bargainable variables. For example, let us suppose that there is just one wage rate in X, and that this wage rate is the *sole* determinant of the quantity of labor demanded by the firm and therefore of employment for the members of the groups. We also suppose that the leadership knows this wage-employment relationship. (It is implied that such things as the level of demand for the employer's product, the shape of that demand curve, technology, the skills of the work force, and the prices of inputs substitutable for and complementary to labor are fixed and will remain so.) Then, employment depends uniquely upon the wage rate, and the group preference orderings over X take this fully into account. In this case, employment need not be included in K. (It is not necessary that the groups know the wage-employment relationship so long as the leadership does know it and also knows the groups' preference orderings over the wage-employment combinations which are allowed by the relationship.)

But if the nonbargainable variable, employment, depends in part upon the wage rate but in part upon changes in product demand and the several other factors mentioned above—and these latter are factors which the union cannot control but about the course of which it can guess with some knowledge—then employment must be included in K. Letting k_1 be employment and x_1 the wage rate, the probability distribution $P(k_1)$ differs depending upon the value of x_1—and thereby of X—achieved.

We have also a relation between X and a distribution of probabilities of various strike lengths. Now any X, or objective, must be: (1) attainable without a strike, in which case $S = 0$, or (2) attainable only after a strike ($S = 1, 2, \ldots$), or (3) unattainable ($X \notin \overset{*}{\mathfrak{X}}$). Therefore for any X, $P(S = 0) + P(S = 1) + P(S = 2) + \cdots + P(X \notin \overset{*}{\mathfrak{X}}) = 1.0$, since $X \in \overset{*}{\mathfrak{X}}$ implies some S, and either $X \in \overset{*}{\mathfrak{X}}$ or $X \notin \overset{*}{\mathfrak{X}}$. If we can suppose the union leadership to have some anticipations about the lengths of strike which the attainment of particular objectives might require, we can also presume it to have anticipations about the likelihoods that certain objectives cannot be obtained at all.

Definition vi.

We now construct the Cartesian product $\mathcal{W} = \mathcal{K} \cdot \mathcal{S}$, where $\mathcal{K} = \{K^{(1)}, K^{(2)}, \ldots\}$ and $\mathcal{S} = \{S^{(1)}, S^{(2)}, \ldots\}$.

Each element in this set consists of one of the possible values of K and one of the possible values of S. These will be designated by double superscripts so that, for example, $W^{11} = (K^{(1)}, S^{(1)})$; $W^{12} = (K^{(1)}, S^{(2)})$; $W^{53} = (K^{(5)}, S^{(3)})$; etc.

Presuming the K's and S's to be independent of each other:

$$P(W^{11}) = P(K^{(1)}) \cdot P(S^{(1)}),$$
$$P(W^{12}) = P(K^{(1)}) \cdot P(S^{(2)}), \text{ etc.}$$

If K and S are dependent, then the likelihood of at least some of the strike lengths will vary as they are associated with different values of K. Then, we must write:

$$P(W^{11}) = P(K^{(1)}) \cdot P_{K^{(1)}}(S^{(1)}), \text{ etc.}$$

Since $P(S^i) = f(X)$ (or, if strike length for a given X depends on K, $P(S^i) = f[X, P(K)]$), we can say $P(W) = F[X, P(K)]$. For any possible bargaining outcome, X^i, once we are given the probability distributions $P_i(k_i)$, then $P[W^{11}(X^i)]$, $P[W^{12}(X^i)]$, etc., are determined. This is true whether or not any of the $P(k_i)$'s are dependent

upon any of the x's, and whether or not any of the $P[S(X^i)]$'s depend on any of the k's. Only if there are no such dependent relationships will the $P(K^i)$'s be the same for all values of X, and the
$P[S(X^i)]$'s the same for all values of K.

It should be noted that $P_{X^i}(W^{11}) + P_{X^i}(W^{12}) + \cdots + P_{X^i}(W^{21}) + P_{X^i}(W^{22}) + \cdots \le 1.0$; and that $1.0 - \Sigma \, P_{X^i}(W^{ij}) = P(X^i \notin \overset{*}{\mathfrak{X}})$.

At this point, it must be recalled (Axiom v) that, should the union
pursue an objective which proves to be unattainable, the "result"
will lie in the nonaffiliation sets of all groups and the union will
cease to exist as a bargaining agent. (The manner of its disappear-
ance might involve the contemporaneous expiration of the firm, the
permanent replacement of the strikers, or the return to work of the
men on an individual basis. Of course, the union might retain some
supporters but would cease to act as the recognized representative of
the workers and as a signatory to their terms of employment.)

For any pair consisting of one objective (X^i) and one group ($G_{j'}$),
the set $\mathcal{W}$ can be partitioned into two subsets. One consists of those
values of W (i.e., of $k_1 \dots k_r$ and of $S(X^i)$) at which X^i would be
sufficiently attractive to cause $G_{j'}$ to remain in the union. This sub-
set we shall call $\overset{*}{\mathcal{W}}(X^i, G_{j'})$. The other subset includes the remaining
values of W. In the event that one of these latter prevails when X^i is
the bargaining outcome, $G_{j'}$ will disaffiliate. When either the outcome or the group is varied, another pair of subsets is created. The
affiliation sets—the $\overset{*}{\mathcal{W}}$'s—corresponding to various groups and outcomes may intersect (indeed it is to be expected that they would),
and some elements in $\mathcal{W}$ may be absent from all of them.

Definition vii.

$$\overset{*}{\mathcal{W}}(X^i, G_{j'}) = \{W \mid W \in \overset{*}{\mathcal{W}}(X^i, G_{j'}) \leftrightarrow G_{j'} \in T\}.$$

For example, $\overset{*}{\mathcal{W}}(X^{(2)}, G_3)$ consists of those pairs (K, S) in $\mathcal{W}$ which,
if $X^{(2)}$ were the bargaining outcome, would imply G_3's (new or con-
tinued) affiliation with T.

Definition viii.

$$\text{Let } \pi_{j'}(X) = P(W(X) \in \overset{*}{\mathcal{W}}_{j'}) = P_X(G_{j'} \in T).$$

For any bargaining objective X^i and group $G_{j'}$, there may be some
values of $W = (K, S)$ which fall in $\overset{*}{\mathcal{W}}(X^i, G_{j'})$. Each such value of W
has a probability $P(W)$ equal to the product $P(K) \cdot P(S)$. $P(K)$
may or may not be independent of the bargaining objective but,
since S is a function of X, the distributions of $P(S)$ and therefore of

$P(W)$ will be different for different objectives. For this reason $\pi_{j'}$, the probability that W is in $\overset{*}{W}_{j'}$, will also be different for different objectives. $\pi_{j'}(X)$ for any objective will be the sum of the probabilities of those W's which fall in $\overset{*}{W}_{j'}$ at that objective.

We can now think of set Π of vectors in which the elements are such probabilities, one for each group.

Definition ix.

$$\Pi = \{\pi \mid \pi = \pi_1(X), \pi_2(X), \ldots \pi_j(X), \ldots \pi_m(X)\}.$$

For example:

$$\pi(X^{(1)}) = \pi_1(X^{(1)}), \pi_2(X^{(1)}), \ldots \pi_j(X^{(1)}), \ldots \pi_m(X^{(1)}).$$

In each such vector, the elements are the probabilities that, in the event of the stipulated outcome, each group will choose affiliation. Thus, $\pi_1(X^{(1)})$ in the above example is the probability that objective $X^{(1)}$ would fall in Group 1's affiliation set, $\pi_2(X^{(1)})$ is the probability that the same objective, $X^{(1)}$, would fall in Group 2's affiliation set, etc. $\pi(X^{(1)})$ is the list of such probabilities for all groups. $\pi(X^{(2)})$ is a similar list for bargaining objective $X^{(2)}$.

Now, let us reformulate the preference ordering for a union trying to win an N.L.R.B.-type election. Given the uncertainty about K and S which we have introduced, the union seeks to maximize the probability of winning such an election.

Definition x.

$$\text{Let } \rho(\pi(X)) = P\left[\sum_{j=1}^{m} (n_j \mid n_j \in T) > \frac{N}{2}\right].$$

Given $\pi(X^{(1)})$, we can calculate the probability, ρ, that, if $X^{(1)}$ should be adopted as the union's policy, a majority of the union's membership would choose affiliation (and the exclusive bargaining rights of the union would be gained or preserved).

Faced with this type of threat, the union's preference ordering may be stated:

$$\rho[\pi(X^{(1)})] > \rho[\pi(X^{(2)})] \longleftrightarrow X^{(1)} >_u X^{(2)};$$
$$\rho[\pi(X^{(1)})] = \rho[\pi(X^{(2)})] \longleftrightarrow X^{(1)} \sim_u X^{(2)}.$$

That is, if $X^{(1)}$ implies a greater probability of winning a representation election than $X^{(2)}$ does, then the union will prefer $X^{(1)}$ to $X^{(2)}$. Should the two probabilities be equal, the union will be indifferent.

We shall use a numerical example similar to the one employed in

Chapter V in order to illustrate this concept. Once again, assume that there are three groups, G_1, G_2, and G_3; and that $n_1/N = 0.4$, $n_2/N = 0.3$, and $n_3/N = 0.3$. To keep the illustration manageable, we shall suppose only three bargaining objectives, two values of S, and two values of K. As a further simplification, K is assumed to be independent of X, and S of K.

Here are the assumed preference orderings of the three groups over $(X, S(X), K)$ and their corresponding affiliation sets; R stands for rank. The symbols, $\in$ and $\notin$, indicate the affiliation and non-affiliation sets of each group. Thus, G_1 will affiliate if one of its seven most preferred situations is achieved, G_2 if one of its top nine, G_3 if one of its top eight.

The preferences have been so set up that $S = 0$ is preferred to $S = 1$ by all groups for any (X, K); similarly, $K^{(1)}$ is preferred to $K^{(2)}$ for any (X, S) by all groups. Preferences among X's (given K and S) differ among the groups.

R	$G_1; \dfrac{n_1}{N} = 0.4$	$G_2; \dfrac{n_2}{N} = 0.3$	$G_3; \dfrac{n_3}{N} = 0.3$
1.	$X^{(2)}, S = 0, K^{(1)} \in$	$X^{(3)}, S = 0, K^{(1)} \in$	$X^{(2)}, S = 0, K^{(1)} \in$
2.	$X^{(1)}, S = 0, K^{(1)} \in$	$X^{(3)}, S = 1, K^{(1)} \in$	$X^{(2)}, S = 0, K^{(2)} \in$
3.	$X^{(2)}, S = 1, K^{(1)} \in$	$X^{(3)}, S = 0, K^{(2)} \in$	$X^{(2)}, S = 1, K^{(1)} \in$
4.	$X^{(1)}, S = 1, K^{(1)} \in$	$X^{(2)}, S = 0, K^{(1)} \in$	$X^{(2)}, S = 1, K^{(2)} \in$
5.	$X^{(2)}, S = 0, K^{(2)} \in$	$X^{(2)}, S = 1, K^{(1)} \in$	$X^{(3)}, S = 0, K^{(1)} \in$
6.	$X^{(1)}, S = 0, K^{(2)} \in$	$X^{(2)}, S = 0, K^{(2)} \in$	$X^{(3)}, S = 0, K^{(2)} \in$
7.	$X^{(3)}, S = 0, K^{(1)} \in$	$X^{(3)}, S = 1, K^{(2)} \in$	$X^{(1)}, S = 0, K^{(1)} \in$
8.	$X^{(2)}, S = 1, K^{(2)} \notin$	$X^{(1)}, S = 0, K^{(1)} \in$	$X^{(1)}, S = 0, K^{(2)} \in$
9.	$X^{(1)}, S = 1, K^{(2)} \notin$	$X^{(1)}, S = 1, K^{(1)} \in$	$X^{(3)}, S = 1, K^{(1)} \notin$
10.	$X^{(3)}, S = 1, K^{(1)} \notin$	$X^{(2)}, S = 1, K^{(2)} \notin$	$X^{(3)}, S = 1, K^{(2)} \notin$
11.	$X^{(3)}, S = 0, K^{(2)} \notin$	$X^{(1)}, S = 0, K^{(2)} \notin$	$X^{(1)}, S = 1, K^{(1)} \notin$
12.	$X^{(3)}, S = 1, K^{(2)} \notin$	$X^{(1)}, S = 1, K^{(2)} \notin$	$X^{(1)}, S = 1, K^{(2)} \notin$
13.	$X^i \notin \mathfrak{X}$ $\notin$	$X^i \notin \mathfrak{X}$ $\notin$	$X^i \notin \mathfrak{X}$ $\notin$

Let the distributions $P(S(X))$ and $P(K)$ be:

K	$P(K)$		X	$S = 0$	$S = 1$	$X \notin \mathfrak{X}$
$K^{(1)}$	0.7		$X^{(1)}$	0.6	0.4	0.0
$K^{(2)}$	0.3		$X^{(2)}$	0.4	0.5	0.1
			$X^{(3)}$	0.2	0.6	0.2

From these distributions we can obtain $P_{x^i}(S(X^i)) \cdot P(K)$ as follows:

K	$X^{(1)}$			$X^{(2)}$			$X^{(3)}$		
	$S = 0$	$S = 1$	$X \notin \mathfrak{X}$	$S = 0$	$S = 1$	$X \notin \mathfrak{X}$	$S = 0$	$S = 1$	$X \notin \mathfrak{X}$
$K^{(1)}$	0.42	0.28	0.00	0.28	0.35	0.07	0.14	0.42	0.14
$K^{(2)}$	0.18	0.12	0.00	0.12	0.15	0.03	0.06	0.18	0.06

We now find $\pi_j(X^i)$:

X	G_1	G_2	G_3
$X^{(1)}$	0.88	0.70	0.60
$X^{(2)}$	0.75	0.75	0.90
$X^{(3)}$	0.14	0.80	0.20

The π's are determined from the groups' preferences and the union's anticipations about S and K. $\pi_1(X^{(1)})$, for example, is the probability that if $X^{(1)}$ is chosen as the union's objective and achieved, then $(X^{(1)}, S(X^{(1)}), K)$ will fall in G_1's affiliation set. That is, $\pi_1(X^{(1)}) = P_{X^{(1)}}(S = 0, K^{(1)}) + P_{X^{(1)}}(S = 1, K^{(1)}) + P_{X^{(1)}}(S = 0, K^{(2)}) = (0.6)(0.7) + (0.4)(0.7) + (0.6)(0.3) = 0.88$. $P_{X^{(1)}}(S = 1, K^{(2)})$, which equals 0.12, is excluded from the sum because $X^{(1)}, S = 1, K^{(2)}$ falls outside of G_1's affiliation set.

To derive the ρ's, and the union's preference ordering, we must note that, in the case of any X^i, some one of the following results must obtain:

(1) $G_1 \in T$ and $G_2 \in T$ and $G_3 \in T$.

(2) $G_1 \in T$ and $G_2 \in T$ and $G_3 \notin T$.

(3) $G_1 \in T$ and $G_2 \notin T$ and $G_3 \in T$.

(4) $G_1 \notin T$ and $G_2 \in T$ and $G_3 \in T$.

(5) $G_1 \in T$ and $G_2 \notin T$ and $G_3 \notin T$.

(6) $G_1 \notin T$ and $G_2 \notin T$ and $G_3 \in T$.

(7) $G_1 \notin T$ and $G_2 \in T$ and $G_3 \notin T$.

(8) $G_1 \notin T$ and $G_2 \notin T$ and $G_3 \notin T$.

The union survival condition is $\sum_{j=1}^m (n_j/N \mid n_j \in T) > 0.5$. Computing $\sum_{j=1}^3 n_j/N \mid n_j \in T$ for each of these eight possibilities, we find that the first four satisfy the condition but that the others do not:

Affiliation results	$\displaystyle\sum_{j=1}^{3} \frac{n_j}{N} \mid n_j \in T$
(1)	1.0
(2)	0.7
(3)	0.7
(4)	0.6
(5)	0.4
(6)	0.3
(7)	0.3
(8)	0.0

Any outcome X^i, then, will be preferred by the union to some other outcome, X^j, only if the probability of affiliation results (1), (2), (3), or (4) is greater in the case of X^i than in the case of X^j.

In the case of $X^{(1)}$ in our example,

$$
\begin{aligned}
\rho(\pi(X^{(1)})) &= \pi_1(X^{(1)}) \cdot \pi_2(X^{(1)}) \cdot \pi_3(X^{(1)}) \\
&+ \pi_1(X^{(1)}) \cdot \pi_2(X^{(1)}) \cdot (1 - \pi_3(X^{(1)})) \\
&+ \pi_1(X^{(1)}) \cdot (1 - \pi_2(X^{(1)})) \cdot \pi_3(X^{(1)}) \\
&+ (1 - \pi_1(X^{(1)})) \cdot \pi_2(X^{(1)}) \cdot \pi_3(X^{(1)}) \\
&= (0.88)(0.70)(0.60) \\
&+ (0.88)(0.70)(0.40) \\
&+ (0.88)(0.30)(0.60) \\
&+ (0.12)(0.70)(0.60) \\
&= 0.3696 + 0.2464 + 0.1584 + 0.0504 = 0.8248.
\end{aligned}
$$

Similar computations yield $\rho(\pi(X^{(2)})) = 0.9000$ and $\rho(\pi(X^{(3)})) = 0.2552$. The union preference ordering, then, will be $X^{(2)} >_u X^{(1)} >_u X^{(3)}$.

A union acting in accord with the hypothesis we have presented would be engaging in maximizing behavior, for the alternative which such a union would choose would be that one for which $\rho(X)$ was greatest. However, two considerations suggest limits to the relevance of our hypothesis. In the first place, where a pair of policies promised approximately the same probabilities of survival, the leadership might not find it worth the effort to seek information about the membership's preferences between the two. By assuming that such information is correct and complete, our model does not really allow for this, but we might say that the union acts as if $\rho(X)$ were an approximate number rounded to, say, the first or second decimal place.

The second limitation of our maximizing hypothesis is a more serious one. Where a union has become quite secure (i.e. where π_j for most or all groups is quite large for many (X, K)), ρ-maximization may be of very limited value in accounting for the choice among bargaining objectives. Many possible alternatives may have been rejected or left unconsidered because they would imply substantial threats to survival, but, if a number of dissimilar outcomes remained, theorizing based on survival needs would not give us a satisfactory explanation of the choice among them. Such supplementary criteria as net revenue maximization or the incumbent leadership's search for continuity in office might be relevant. Hypotheses about the behavior of unions in which threats to leadership survival are significant are advanced in a later section. At this point, we shall make a formal statement, which will be of some use later, of the limitation of the union-survival hypothesis we might expect in a secure union.

Let $\mathring{\rho}$ be some value of $\rho(X)$. We can think of it as a "satisfactory" probability of survival, so high that the leadership acts as if the union is "safe," even though $\mathring{\rho}$ may be less than 1.0. When $\rho(X) < \mathring{\rho}$, our hypothesis is presumed to apply. To explain the union's preference ordering among $X \mid \rho(X) > \mathring{\rho}$, some supplementary hypothesis is required. Formally:

Axiom vi.

$$\rho(X^{(1)}) < \mathring{\rho}$$

or

$$\rho(X^{(2)}) < \mathring{\rho} \;\leftrightarrow\; \{[\rho(X^{(1)}) > \rho(X^{(2)})] \leftrightarrow (X^{(1)} >_u X^{(2)})\}$$

and

$$\{[\rho(X^{(1)}) = \rho(X^{(2)})] \leftrightarrow (X^{(1)} \sim_u X^{(2)})\}.$$

That is, only if one or both of the alternatives lie below $\mathring{\rho}$ will the hypothesis which we have advanced necessarily explain the union's preference ordering between them.

Another kind of threat to union survival, one which may lead to a union preference ordering differing from those developed so far, is posed by the possibility of loss of an organizational strike. Here there is no statutory or other external determination of the union's representational rights, and no statutory requirement that the employer bargain with a majority union. The acquisition and preservation of representational rights depend upon forcing the employer to negotiate in the face of the union's threat to cause a costly cessation of production if he does not. If the union is to bring production to a halt, it must be able to command the allegiance in a strike of those workers who are essential to that production. It is presumed that the employer is legally free to replace strikers and that both replacements and capitulating strikers are legally and physically free to work if they wish to. Among the workers involved, some can be readily replaced by the employer while others cannot. Those who are not readily replaceable are those performing work essential to production when: (1) the costs of training other workers in these skills (including profit opportunities foregone during the training period) are, from the firm's point of view, prohibitive; and (2) no adequate supply of trained replacements is available. The latter condition may exist because of a tight labor market or because the craft is completely organized. We shall continue to use the description of the union and the conceptual apparatus already developed, and to presume the union leadership to have perfect knowledge of the preference orderings of the groups but to be uncertain about values of K and S. As a result of this uncertainty the union acts as if there were probability distributions $P(K)$ and $P(S(X))$. From these distributions we derive, as before, the distribution $P(W(X))$, where $W^{ij} = (K^i, S^j)$. Any combination, (X, W), implies for each group either $G_j \in T$ or $G_j \notin T$. $\overset{*}{W}(X', G_j')$ is the subset of W containing all the values and only the values of W which—in the case of the objective X' and the group G_j'—imply $G_j' \in T$. Each X^i implies a unique distribution, $P(W)$. Therefore each X^i implies for each group a unique value, $P_X{}^i(W \in \overset{*}{W}_j')$, which can also be written $P_{X^i}(G_j' \in T)$ or $\pi_j'(X^i)$.

While the logical relations among these concepts are retained, it is necessary to reinterpret some of them so as to fit the new situation. The union is concerned both with acquiring or keeping representational rights and with obtaining a contract covering wages and other bargainable variables. The set of attainable outcomes (contracts) may include some which can be achieved without any strike. Others can be won only if those workers whose services are essential to production are willing to stay out on strike long enough to get them. Unattainable outcomes, as before, are those which the employer would never yield.

The threat to the union's position as bargaining agent comes from two directions. On the one hand, if the union asks for too much—in the sense of an objective implying a strike longer than the workers are willing to undergo—the "essentials" will disaffiliate by returning to work on a unilateral basis (or, perhaps, as a "company union") against the union's orders; the strike and the union both collapse. The act of disaffiliation then occurs during the bargaining, not at some later time. When S reaches a magnitude such that $(X, S(X), K)$ falls outside of $G_{j'}$'s affiliation set, then $G_{j'}$ disaffiliates by returning to work.

On the other hand, the union may ask for "too little." An agreement reached without a strike, for example, might yield so little utility for the essential members as to lead to their disaffiliation in another way. Disappointed by an outcome which, to them, makes the union not worth having, they manifest their discontent by withholding dues, by joining a rival union, or simply by grumbling. If this behavior actually indicates disaffiliation (rather than, say, only lack of support for the union's present leadership), the employer may withdraw recognition from the union with impunity. For the union could retain recognition only by means of a strike in which the disgruntled "essentials" are now unwilling to engage.

These considerations suggest that the strike length function, rather than the k's, is in this case the crucial determinant of whether the union survives or goes under. Since the issue is apt to be decided quickly, the dispersion of the probability distributions of many of the k's may be smaller than in the certification election case. For instance, large changes in the general level of retail prices are less likely to occur during a strike of days or weeks than in the longer period after the signing of an agreement during which a certification election might take place. On the other hand, some k's might be relatively important and difficult to predict in a situation of this kind. For example, the amount (if any) of public funds which local authorities were willing to disburse as relief payments to strikers and their families, and the extent to which local merchants would extend credit to strikers, could both be of considerable importance.

Three observations about the nature and frequency of the kind of organizational strikes with which we are concerned appear to be in order.

First, by "organizational strike" is meant a strike in which recognition of the union as the bargaining representative of the workers is an issue. It may be that the union has never before been recognized or on the other hand that a union currently enjoying bargaining rights faces the threat that recognition will be withdrawn.

Second, the hypothesis offered does not purport to deal with all types of organizational strikes. It is concerned only with those cases in which the union's success or failure in obtaining recognition, along with an agreement, depends entirely upon the refusal of certain "essential" employees to return to work until the agreement is won. At least two methods of obtaining recognition, in addition to the electoral method discussed above, are excluded from the analysis. These are: (1) obtaining recognition through secondary pressure, in which the union's success depends upon the actions of allies or "conscripted neutrals," and (2) obtaining recognition by mass picketing. Where effective mass picketing—that is, picketing in sufficient numbers to prevent entrance onto the employer's premises—is permitted by the authorities, the union can interrupt production so long as it commands enough supporters to make the picketing effective, whoever these supporters may be.

Third, since the imposition upon a large number of employers of the statutory duty to bargain, organizational strikes have declined as a percentage of all strikes.[1] They still occur, however; strikes over recognition (certification), recognition and job security, recognition and economic issues, and refusal to sign agreements accounted for an average of 8.8% of work stoppages classified annually by the U.S. Department of Labor in the years 1964 through 1968 inclusive.[2] A considerable sector of our economy remains outside of the jurisdictions of the N.L.R.B. and of the few state agencies which perform similar functions.

The danger to the union's existence under the conditions with which this section is concerned differs from the one dealt with earlier. Consequently a new symbol, ρ', derived below, is introduced to stand for the probability that a union will survive when threatened with the possible loss of an organizational strike.

Definition x (b).
Let $\mathring{G}$ be the set of all possible subsets of G.

Let V be a subset of $\mathring{G}$. V should be interpreted as referring to the subset of $\mathring{G}$ which contains all those subsets of G, the affiliation of which with the union implies its survival.

---

[1] W. S. Woytinsky and Associates, *Employment and Wages in the United States* (New York: Twentieth Century Fund, 1953), Table 59, p. 654.

[2] U. S. Bureau of Labor Statistics, *Handbook of Labor Statistics, 1970,* Bulletin 1666 (Washington: U. S. Government Printing Office), Table 156, pp. 344–348.

Let $\rho'[\pi(X)] = P[(\text{all } G'_j \mid G'_j \in T) \in V]$.
The union's preference ordering will be:

$$X^{(1)} >_u X^{(2)} \longleftrightarrow \rho'[\pi(X^{(1)})] > \rho'[\pi(X^{(2)})].$$

$$X^{(1)} \sim_u X^{(2)} \longleftrightarrow \rho'[\pi(X^{(1)})] = \rho'[\pi(X^{(2)})].$$

Once again, we shall use a numerical example to illustrate this particular resolution of divergent membership objectives. Suppose once more that there are three groups and three objectives; that the group preference orderings and affiliation sets, and the distributions $P(K)$ and $P(S(X))$ are the same as those on page 127 above. (These assumptions are made for the sake of convenience, but it should be remembered that affiliation of a group in the representation election sense need not imply affiliation of that group in the strike support sense in which the relationship $G_j \in T$ is used in this section.) Indeed, because the costs and risks incurred by workers in a recognition strike are relatively large, we would expect the $\pi_j(X^i)$'s typically to be smaller in the present context than in the previous one.) By assumption, then, the values of $\pi_j(X)$ for each group are the same as in the earlier example, namely:

X	G_1	G_2	G_3
$X^{(1)}$	0.88	0.70	0.60
$X^{(2)}$	0.75	0.75	0.90
$X^{(3)}$	0.14	0.80	0.20

To compute ρ' for these three outcomes, the indices $n_j \mid N$ are no longer important. We must know which groups are irreplaceable by the employer and essential to production (and therefore also essential to the stoppage of that production and the winning of an organizational strike.) We shall suppose that in order to operate its facilities the firm needs G_1 and either G_2 or G_3. (The latter part of our assumption would be plausible if G_2 and G_3 each contained enough trained individuals to assure the performance of certain essential tasks.)

$\mathcal{G}$ consists of $\{G_1, G_2, G_3\}$, and $\mathring{G}$ is composed of:

(1) G_1, G_2, G_3.   (5) G_1.

(2) G_1, G_3.   (6) G_2.

(3) G_2, G_3.   (7) G_3.

(4) G_1, G_2.   (8) Λ.

To defeat the union, the employer needs G_1 and either G_2 or G_3. To win its strike, then, the union needs either G_1 (alone or along with other groups) or both G_2 and G_3. Consequently, V includes the subsets in $\overset{\circ}{G}$ numbered (1) through (5), above.

$$\rho'[\pi(X^{(1)})],$$

then, equals:

$$P_{X^{(1)}}(G_1 \in T \text{ and } G_2 \in T \text{ and } G_3 \in T)$$
$$+ P_{X^{(1)}}(G_1 \in T \text{ and } G_2 \notin T \text{ and } G_3 \in T)$$
$$+ P_{X^{(1)}}(G_1 \notin T \text{ and } G_2 \in T \text{ and } G_3 \in T)$$
$$+ P_{X^{(1)}}(G_1 \in T \text{ and } G_2 \in T \text{ and } G_3 \notin T)$$
$$+ P_{X^{(1)}}(G_1 \in T \text{ and } G_2 \notin T \text{ and } G_3 \notin T)$$

$$= \pi_1(X^{(1)}) \cdot \pi_2(X^{(1)}) \cdot \pi_3(X^{(1)})$$
$$+ \pi_1(X^{(1)}) \cdot (1 - \pi_2(X^{(1)})) \cdot \pi_3(X^{(1)})$$
$$+ (1 - \pi_1(X^{(1)})) \cdot \pi_2(X^{(1)}) \cdot \pi_3(X^{(1)})$$
$$+ \pi_1(X^{(1)}) \cdot \pi_2(X^{(1)}) \cdot (1 - \pi_3(X^{(1)}))$$
$$+ \pi_1(X^{(1)}) \cdot (1 - \pi_2(X^{(1)})) \cdot (1 - \pi_3(X^{(1)})).$$

Filling in the values of $\pi_j(X^{(1)})$ in the last expression, we have:

$$
\begin{aligned}
\rho'(X^{(1)}) = \ & (.088)(0.70)(0.60) \\
+ \ & (0.88)(0.30)(0.60) \\
+ \ & (0.12)(0.70)(0.60) \\
+ \ & (0.88)(0.70)(0.40) \\
+ \ & (0.88)(0.30)(0.40) \\
= \ & 0.3696 + 0.1584 + 0.0504 + 0.2464 + 0.1056 = 0.9304.
\end{aligned}
$$

Similar computations yield $\rho'(X^{(2)}) = 0.19875$ and $\rho'(X^{(3)}) = 0.2776$.

The preference ordering most compatible with union survival, then, is:

$$X^{(1)} >_u X^{(2)} >_u X^{(3)}.$$

Faced with identical π_j's, our hypothetical union's preference ordering was changed when we altered the survival criterion. In the representation election case, $X^{(2)} >_u X^{(1)}$, but in the organizational strike case $X^{(1)} >_u X^{(2)}$. Among the groups, only for G_1 is $\pi(X^{(1)}) > \pi(X^{(2)})$. It is G_1's importance to both employer and union in the case of an organizational strike which had the effect of altering the union's preference ordering.

As before, there may be some probability of union survival so high that the leadership acts as if the union were "safe." Let $\mathring{\rho}'$ stand for such a probability in the present case.

Axiom vi (b):

Let $\mathring{\rho}'$ be some value of $\rho'(X)$.

The union's preference ordering over alternative bargaining outcomes in this case is:

$$\rho'(X^{(1)}) < \mathring{\rho}'$$

or

$$\rho'(X^{(2)}) < \mathring{\rho}' \leftrightarrow X^{(1)} >_u X^{(2)} \leftrightarrow \rho'[\pi(X^{(1)})] > \rho'[\pi(X^{(2)})]$$

and

$$X^{(1)} \sim_u X^{(2)} \leftrightarrow \rho'[\pi(X^{(1)})] = \rho'[\pi(X^{(2)})].$$

For bargaining outcomes with $\rho' > \mathring{\rho}'$, the union may be concerned with maximizing net revenue, reducing employer hostility, or other secondary goals.

Chapter VII

FURTHER EXPLORATIONS

We turn now to the preference ordering of the union leadership confronted by the possibility of ouster from office. One version of this situation—in which an opposition is already established—was analyzed earlier (in Chapter IV), but under the simpler conditions of certainty about the values of the k's and of $S(X)$, and with a single bargainable variable. In that context, competition between organizational security and leadership security was not possible. An objective either promised union survival or it did not; it promised leadership survival or it did not; and unless one or the other of these aims was impossible, there would be at least one objective promising both. Now, however, we are dealing with many variables in a probabilistic setting. Very often, one objective will be superior to another on both counts. But situations may arise where the chances of forestalling a rival union can be enhanced at the expense of increasing an internal threat to the leadership, and vice versa. There are two ways of adjusting our model to cope with this. One of these is to treat leadership survival as a criterion which determines preference orderings only among possible outcomes which promise safe probabilities of union survival.

This is illustrated in the form of an indifference map in Figure 7-1, where $\rho(X^i)$ stands for the probability that X^i will lead to union survival and $R(X^i)$ for the probability that X^i will lead to leadership survival. Any objective yielding a higher ρ is preferred to any objective yielding a lower ρ so long as $\rho < \mathring{\rho}$. When $\rho \geq \mathring{\rho}$, preferences are based on R.

A second approach would allow for some substitutability between ρ and R, especially (and perhaps only) at moderate values of each, as in Figure 7-2. For the time being, we shall work with the simpler formulation (7-1).

In analyzing preference orderings based on probabilities of leadership survival, two kinds of threats to incumbent officeholders may be distinguished. In the first and, among national unions in the U.S., rarer case there is an established opposition which can be expected to offer alternative candidates for the elective offices.

The leadership faces a somewhat different threat when there is no established opposition but only the possibility that one might develop if an important segment of the membership were to become

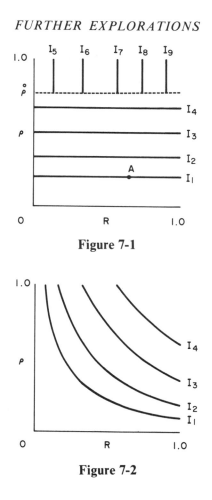

Figure 7-1

Figure 7-2

sufficiently disaffected with the incumbents. Just as the presence of a rival union makes disaffiliation easier, the existence of an opposition party facilitates overthrow of the leadership. The coordinated efforts required to construct an opposition are greater than those necessary to vote for an existing one. Where there is no organized opposition, the leadership is free to pursue some policies which would be dangerous or even untenable if a second party were on hand to attack them. But this advantage will be kept only so long as the policies followed are acceptable enough to prevent such an opposition from arising.

Some observations are in order before we proceed with the formal analysis of these two cases in which the leadership's quest for continuance in office provides the criterion upon which the union's policy decisions are based.

The leadership, in seeking the members' endorsement, must deal with a universe of "policy variables" of which the bargainable variables may be only a part. Internal policy matters may be of crucial importance. Such matters as the issuing of permits, the handling of union funds, the level of dues, respect for another union's picket lines, or the racial distribution of union jobs may assume considerable significance. The day-to-day administration of the contract—the results of grievance processing—may also be of great importance. While contract administration is bargaining of a sort, the variables involved do not quite fit our earlier conception of the bargaining objectives as a set of terms embodied in a written collective agreement. Our formal analysis does not extend to these matters. In presenting hypotheses suggesting that the leadership will in some circumstances choose that bargaining objective most conducive to its reelection, we do not imply that the bargaining outcome is the only factor affecting the leadership's chances.

In referring to the "leadership" we mean, as before, the effective makers of policy. In some cases the elected officers are split, some being in a majority slate seeking retention while the remainder lead an opposition seeking to assume control. In such situations the term "leadership" refers to the majority faction.

Where there is an established opposition, the leadership's preference ordering of attainable outcomes may be similar to that of the union facing potential defeat in a representation election. The leadership is faced with the task of framing a bargaining policy which will be one of the determinants of its success or failure in achieving reelection at some later date. The relevant values of the k's, then, are those which occur between the signing of the agreement and the subsequent election. But in the case with which we are now concerned, the election is an internal one.

Several minor changes in the logical structure developed earlier are necessary. First, since the electorate consists of the union membership, we replace E—the work force over which the union has or seeks bargaining rights—with T, the union. Hence, Definition i is altered in part to read, $G_1 \cup G_2 \cup \ldots \cup G_j \cup \ldots \cup G_m = T$ (rather than E). Second, the kind of "disaffiliation" which now concerns us is repudiation of an incumbent leadership rather than of the union itself. The symbol A ("administration") will be used to signify the incumbent leadership, and the statement, "$G_j \in A$," will mean:

"The j'th group will vote for the leadership slate." For reasons which will not become clear until later, two of our axioms must be dropped for our analysis of the preference ordering of the leadership faced by an internal opposition. These are Axioms iii and iv (Chapter V, page 106), which state that if alternative $(X, K)^{(1)}$ implies a group's affiliation while $(X, K)^{(2)}$ does not, then the group in question must prefer $(X, K)^{(1)}$ to $(X, K)^{(2)}$. This need not apply to affiliation with A. Otherwise, our definitions and axioms—with proper notational adjustment—still stand.

We must also define a new set, $\overline{W}(X^i, G_j')$, playing the same role as that of $\overset{*}{W}(X^i, G_j')$ in our earlier analysis. Let $\overline{W}(X^i, G_j') = \{W \mid W \in \overline{W}(X^i, G_j') \leftrightarrow (G_j' \in A)\}$. Thus, $\overline{W}(X^{(2)}, G_3)$ includes those pairs (K, S) in W which, if $X^{(2)}$ were the bargaining outcome, would imply G_3's affiliation (via favorable votes) with A.

Replacement of $\pi_{j'}(X)$ with the probability that $G_{j'}$ will vote for the incumbents is also required.

$$\text{Let } \lambda_{j'}(X) = P(W(X) \in \overline{W}_{j'}) = P_X(G_{j'} \in A).$$

The set of vectors of such affiliation probabilities, $L = \{\lambda \mid \lambda = \lambda_1(X), \lambda_2(X), \ldots \lambda_j(X), \ldots \lambda_m(X)\}$.

All of these notational alterations are only formal manifestations of our shift of attention from the matter of affiliation with a union to that of support of an incumbent leadership. From these revisions it follows that $N = \sum_{j=1}^m n_j$ is now the number of individuals in T rather than in E.

$$\text{Let } R(\lambda(X)) = P\left[\sum_{j=1}^m \quad (n_j \mid n_j \in A) > \frac{N}{2} \right].$$

In a union faced by the possibility of dispossesion through a representation election, and also characterized internally by an established opposition expected to attempt the overthrow of the incumbent administration at the next election, the union's preference ordering might be as follows:

$$(\rho(X^{(2)}) < \overset{\circ}{\rho}) \rightarrow \{[\rho(X^{(1)}) > \rho(X^{(2)})] \rightarrow [X^{(1)} >_u X^{(2)}]\}.$$
$$\{\rho(X^{(1)}) \geq \overset{\circ}{\rho} \text{ and } \rho(X^{(2)}) \geq \overset{\circ}{\rho}\}$$
$$\rightarrow \{[R(X^{(1)}) > R(X^{(2)})] \leftrightarrow [X^{(1)} >_u X^{(2)}]\}.$$

This is the model illustrated by Figure 7-1, in which union survival takes priority over leadership reelection.

It also seems reasonable to suppose that, for values of $\rho(X)$ below

$\overset{\circ}{\rho}$, of two outcomes promising equal chances of union survival the one most conducive to the leadership's reelection would be preferred. Thus we can add:

$$\{\rho(X^{(1)}) < \overset{\circ}{\rho} \text{ and } \rho(X^{(2)}) < \overset{\circ}{\rho} \text{ and } \rho(X^{(1)}) = \rho(^{(2)})\} \longleftrightarrow$$
$$\{[R(X^{(1)}) > R(X^{(2)})] \longleftrightarrow [X^{(1)} >_u X^{(2)}]\}.$$

Incidentally, this last condition is not completely consistent with Figure 7-1, as far as the horizontal indifference curves are concerned. Rather, it implies that, on any of the horizontal lines such as I_1, a point such as A is preferred to all points on I_1 to its left, while all points on I_1 to the right of A are preferred to A.

Finally, there are two circumstances in which the union will be indifferent.

$$\{\rho(X^{(1)}) < \overset{\circ}{\rho} \text{ and } \rho(X^{(2)}) < \overset{\circ}{\rho} \text{ and } \rho(X^{(1)}) = \rho(X^{(2)})\} \longrightarrow$$
$$\{[R(X^{(1)}) = R(X^{(2)})] \longleftrightarrow [X^{(1)} \sim_u X^{(2)}]\}.$$
$$\{\rho(X^{(1)}) > \overset{\circ}{\rho} \text{ and } \rho(X^{(2)}) > \overset{\circ}{\rho}\} \longrightarrow \{[R(X^{(1)}) = R(X^{(2)})] \longleftrightarrow$$
$$[X^{(1)} \sim_u X^{(2)}]\}.$$

It may be that union survival and leadership survival are competing criteria as in Figure 7-2. To say that they are competing criteria means that:

(a) there is at least one pair of bargaining objectives, $X^{(1)}$ and $X^{(2)}$, such that $X^{(1)}$ implies $(R^{(1)}, \rho^{(1)})$ and $X^{(2)}$ implies $(R^{(2)}, \rho^{(2)})$;

(b) the values of $(R^{(1)}, \rho^{(1)})$ and $(R^{(2)}, \rho^{(2)})$ are such that $R^{(1)} > R^{(2)}$ while $\rho^{(1)} < \rho^{(2)}$; and

(c) $X^{(1)} \sim_u X^{(2)}$.

In such a case the union preference orderings are based on some function—call it ϕ—of R and ρ, and:

$$\phi(X^{(1)}) > \phi(X^{(2)}) \longleftrightarrow X^{(1)} >_u X^{(2)},$$

while

$$\phi(X^{(1)}) = \phi(X^{(2)}) \longleftrightarrow X^{(1)} \sim_u X^{(2)}.$$

So far, our formulation of the preferences of a leadership threatened from within bypasses one aspect of the situation which it describes. Whether or not an outcome X^i falls, under particular circumstances, in some group's A-affiliation set $\overline{W}$ depends not just on what K and S turn out to be but also on what the opposition says it would have done. Let us suppose, as in Chapter IV, that the opposition will pick the platform with the greatest vote-potential. It is this consideration which is responsible for the abandonment, mentioned above, of Axiom iii in our treatment of internal rivalry. Suppose that, for the j'th group, $X^{(3)} >_j X^{(1)} >_j X^{(2)} >_j X^{(4)}$. Preferences of the other groups might be such that if $X^{(1)}$ were the bargaining outcome, the opposition would champion $X^{(3)}$, while an outcome of $X^{(2)}$ would lead it to proclaim that it would have obtained $X^{(4)}$. Thus it is possible that even though $X^{(1)} >_j X^{(2)}$, $X^{(1)} \rightarrow (G_j \notin A)$, while $X^{(2)} \rightarrow (G_j \in A)$.

The dependence of affiliation sets on the strategy of an assumedly opportunistic opposition underlies the following discussion of the constraints which such an opposition's existence will exert on leadership behavior.

In Chapter IV, where—under conditions of certainty—group preferences about the wage rate and strike lengths were presumed to behave according to certain rules, it was demonstrated that the existence of an established opposition might limit the number of alternatives among which the leadership could choose without fear of ouster. At the extreme, assuming the bargaining outcome to be the sole issue at stake in a future union election, the incumbents would be forced to a specific solution, the majority wage, as a condition of retaining office. Fear of the opposition would then function as a close substitute for a requirement of majority ratification of any proposed agreement. In Chapter V, our model was expanded to allow for any number of bargainable variables; and all constraints on group preference orderings save the rule of transitivity were removed, although the assumption of certainty was continued. In discussing the effects of a membership ratification requirement, we showed that in our expanded model there might or might not be a unique majority objective, X_m, corresponding to our earlier majority wage. If there were no such objective there would at least be a set of objectives, $[X_m]$, preferred by a majority to all others. The objectives in this set were characterized as having intransitive majority rank-ordering relations with each other. (The composition of the majority, of course, differs for each comparison between a pair of alternatives in $[X_m]$.) We then showed how a decision would be reached, our results depending upon our assumptions about the groups' knowledge of each others' preferences and on the temporal order in which solutions in $[X_m]$ became available.

The same analysis, assuming many bargainable variables but with certainty about K and S as in Chapter V, may be applied to the case of rivalry between incumbent and opposition factions. If there is a unique X_m, the incumbents must settle for it. If there is not, they must certainly settle for one of the outcomes in $[X_m]$. But, supposing still that there are no election issues save the bargaining outcome and also that the opposition is free to advocate retrospectively any alternative outcome to the one actually achieved, will not the absence of a unique X_m guarantee an opposition victory? For, assuming the negotiations to precede the election, the incumbents will necessarily settle for some X^i in $[X_m]$. There must be some X^j in $[X_m]$ which a majority prefers to X^i. (Otherwise, X^i would be a unique majority objective.) All the opposition needs to get elected is to identify X^j and proclaim that they would have obtained it— provided that the electorate views the contest entirely in terms of X^i vs. X^j.

An electorate aware of the implications of intransitivity in majority rank-ordering might not vote this way. Such awareness, incidentally, does not presume understanding of the definition of intransitivity any more than Machlup's motorist[1] needed to know the laws of physics or the engineering of his vehicle. What it does require is that the voter know something of the preferences of groups other than his own. He may then conclude, for example, that the incumbents have done a reasonably good job, that no policy would be regarded as "best" by everyone, that the opposition can be expected to play upon various discontents but cannot be expected, once in office, to behave much better or worse than the incumbents have been doing. Perhaps the incumbents will be able to obtain reelection so long as they pick some objective in $[X_m]$ if the union's members are well informed about each other's preferences and react in the manner of the hypothetical member cited above.

Actual elections, of course, may be determined in part on questions of internal administration or of the handling of grievances; and success in such matters may give the incumbents some leeway. If we ignore these last considerations, however, an established opposition which is free after the conclusion of negotiations to pick as its platform any X^i other than the one actually achieved will push the leadership to some outcome in the majority set $[X_m]$. Our formulation assumes that the opposition must advocate the same platform before all groups: if it does not approximate such a position, the incumbents may be expected to point out its inconsistencies.

---

[1] Fritz Machlup, "Marginal Analysis and Empirical Research," *American Economic Review*, XXXVI (September 1946), pp. 534–535.

But once we introduce uncertainty about K and S into our model, the leadership can no longer be sure just which bargaining objectives will be in the majority set. Let us suppose once again that the union election will occur after a bargaining objective has been achieved, and that the election will depend on the members' preferences as between the objective actually obtained and that which the opposition advocates. The latter objective is still assumed to be the one which will yield it the greatest number of votes. The choice is between the (X^i, K, S) actually achieved and the X^j which the opposition advocates, given the probabilities—as the voters appraise them—that various values of K and S would have occurred had X^j in fact been the policy pursued. The leadership's road to reelection lies in choosing that bargaining objective which promises the best chance of being preferred by a majority to the alternative which the opposition advances.

The following example is intended to clarify the problem and to present a solution.

We shall suppose that there are three groups, any two of which constitute a majority of the union electorate, and that there are three possible values of X. To keep our example manageable, we suppose that the future value of K is given; uncertainty concerning strike lengths will suffice to distinguish this analysis from earlier ones. We shall limit ourselves to three bargaining objectives and two strike lengths, and assume the preferences of the groups to be:

Table 7-1

Rank	G_1	G_2	G_3
1	$X^{(2)}, S = 0$	$X^{(3)}, S = 0$	$X^{(2)}, S = 0$
2	$X^{(1)}, S = 0$	$X^{(3)}, S = 1$	$X^{(1)}, S = 0$
3	$X^{(2)}, S = 1$	$X^{(2)}, S = 0$	$X^{(3)}, S = 0$
4	$X^{(1)}, S = 1$	$X^{(2)}, S = 1$	$X^{(2)}, S = 1$
5	$X^{(3)}, S = 0$	$X^{(1)}, S = 0$	$X^{(1)}, S = 1$
6	$X^{(3)}, S = 1$	$X^{(1)}, S = 1$	$X^{(3)}, S = 1$

The $P(S)$ distributions, as seen by the leadership, are:

Table 7-2

Objective	$P(S = 0)$	$P(S = 1)$
$X^{(1)}$	0.7	0.3
$X^{(2)}$	0.2	0.8
$X^{(3)}$	0.5	0.5

The reader should note that the preferences described in Table 7-1 are so drawn up as to produce, *at any given strike length,* a transitive majority rank ordering, with $X^{(2)} >_m X^{(1)} >_m X^{(3)}$. But the fact that the strike length is uncertain rules out the possibility that the leadership can avoid all chance of ouster by choosing $X^{(2)}$ as its goal.

Table 7-1 did not include the A-affiliation sets of the groups. In other contexts, we have postulated these arbitrarily. But here—under the assumption that the election will test sentiment on the bargaining outcome alone—these affiliation sets can be partially, but not entirely, derived from the group preferences (Table 7-1) and the presumed opportunism of the opposition. The affiliation data which we can infer are shown in Table 7-3. For example, suppose that $(X^{(1)}, S = 1)$ is the outcome and that the opposition says that it would have fought for $X^{(3)}$. Table 7-1 makes it clear that Group G_1 prefers $(X^{(1)}, S = 1)$ to $X^{(3)}$ obtained under any circumstances and will vote for ($\in$) the incumbent administration. G_2's preferences are in this respect the reverse of G_1's, and it will vote for the opposition candidates ($\notin$). But what about Group 3? The answer is not clear, for $(X^{(3)}, S = 0) >_3 (X^{(1)}, S = 1) >_3 (X^{(3)}, S = 1)$. Hence, a question mark has been placed in the appropriate location in Table 7-3.

Table 7-3

If outcome is:	And opposition claims it would have sought:								
	$X^{(1)}$			$X^{(2)}$			$X^{(3)}$		
	Group affiliation sets will be:								
	G_1	G_2	G_3	G_1	G_2	G_3	G_1	G_2	G_3
$X^{(1)}, S = 0$	—	—	—	?	$\notin$	?	$\in$	$\notin$	$\in$
$X^{(1)}, S = 1$	—	—	—	$\notin$	$\notin$	$\notin$	$\in$	$\notin$	?
$X^{(2)}, S = 0$	$\in$	$\in$	$\in$	—	—	—	$\in$	$\notin$	$\in$
$X^{(2)}, S = 1$	?	$\in$	?	—	—	—	$\in$	$\notin$	?
$X^{(3)}, S = 0$	$\notin$	$\in$	?	$\notin$	$\in$	?	—	—	—
$X^{(3)}, S = 1$	$\notin$	$\in$	$\notin$	$\notin$	$\in$	$\notin$	—	—	—

The Group affiliation sets, then, can be but partially inferred from the given data, and, in order to determine the choice of objective which a survival-oriented leadership should make, we must complete them by assumption. Consider G_3's dilemma, mentioned above, if faced with an accomplished outcome of $(X^{(1)}, S = 1)$ and an opposition claiming that it would have worked for $X^{(3)}$. Our approach to this problem is suggested by Luce and Raiffa's exposition of von Neumann-Morgenstern utility.[2] G_3 is faced with two alternatives. One is the achieved outcome, $(X^{(1)}, S = 1)$. The other is some probability, p, that a superior result—$(X^{(3)}, S = 0)$—would have been achieved if the opposition had been in power; *and* another probability, $1 - p$, that an inferior result—$(X^{(3)}, S = 1)$—would have occurred. G_3's choice depends on these probabilities and on how it feels about the relative superiority and inferiority of the outcomes to which they are attached. G_3's ex post estimate of the probability that $X^{(3)}$ could have been achieved without a strike need not equal the leadership's ex ante estimate of 0.5. Indeed, the opposition will try to push G_3's estimate of this value toward unity while administration campaigners seek to drag it toward zero. But, since we have to make some assumptions about these probabilities, we shall suppose that all the necessary ex post Group estimates of $P[S(X)]$ are equal to the leadership's ex ante estimates in Table 7-2.

Now, we shall eliminate the eight question marks in Table 7-3 by making assumptions about group preferences. These will be arbitrary in the sense that they cannot be inferred from anything which has been presented before. After eliminating some of the question marks by assumption, we shall resolve others by invoking our rule that Group preference orderings must be transitive. For G_1, we postulate that:

$$(X^{(1)}, S = 0) > [0.2(X^{(2)}, S = 0); 0.8(X^{(2)}, S = 1)].$$
$$[0.7(X^{(1)}, S = 0); 0.3(X^{(1)}, S = 1)] > (X^{(2)}, S = 1).$$

And for G_3, we postulate that:

$$(X^{(3)}, S = 0) > [0.2(X^{(2)}, S = 0); 0.8(X^{(2)}, S = 1)].$$
$$[0.7(X^{(1)}, S = 0); 0.3(X^{(1)}, S = 1)] > (X^{(3)}, S = 0).$$
$$(X^{(2)}, S = 1) > [0.5(X^{(3)}, S = 0); 0.5(X^{(3)}, S = 1)].$$
$$[0.5(X^{(3)}, S = 0); 0.5(X^{(3)}, S = 1)] > (X^{(1)}, S = 1).$$

It is now implied that, for G_3:

$$(X^{(1)}, S = 0) > [0.2(X^{(2)}, S = 0); 0.8(X^{(2)}, S = 1)].$$
$$[0.7(X^{(1)}, S = 0); 0.3(X^{(1)}, S = 1)] > (X^{(2)}, S = 1).$$

Table 7-3A shows us the completed affiliation sets of the Groups.

[2]R. Duncan Luce and Howard Raiffa, *Games and Decisions: Introduction and Critical Survey* (New York: John Wiley and Sons, 1957), pp. 19–34.

Table 7-3A

If outcome is:	And opposition claims it would have sought:								
	$X^{(1)}$			$X^{(2)}$			$X^{(3)}$		
	Group affiliation sets will be:								
	G_1	G_2	G_3	G_1	G_2	G_3	G_1	G_2	G_3
$X^{(1)}, S = 0$	—	—	—	$\in$	$\notin$	$\in$	$\in$	$\notin$	$\in$
$X^{(1)}, S = 1$	—	—	—	$\notin$	$\notin$	$\notin$	$\in$	$\notin$	$\notin$
$X^{(2)}, S = 0$	$\in$	$\in$	$\in$	—	—	—	$\in$	$\notin$	$\in$
$X^{(2)}, S = 1$	$\notin$	$\in$	$\notin$	—	—	—	$\in$	$\notin$	$\in$
$X^{(3)}, S = 0$	$\notin$	$\in$	$\notin$	$\notin$	$\in$	$\in$	—	—	—
$X^{(3)}, S = 1$	$\notin$	$\in$	$\notin$	$\notin$	$\in$	$\notin$	—	—	—

Although the next step is not necessary, it is included to illustrate the concept of "λ," and to show that the values of λ depend on opposition strategy. For each possible bargaining objective and each possible opposition platform (i.e. another bargaining objective), Table 7-4 shows the λ's—the probabilities for each group that it would vote for the administration. These are based entirely on the affiliation sets in Table 7-3A and the $P(S)$ distributions in Table 7-2. For example, suppose that the incumbents pursue and achieve $X^{(1)}$ and that the opposition is expected to advance (later, in the election campaign) $X^{(2)}$ as the objective which it would have sought. Table 7-3A tells us that if $X^{(1)}$ is achieved with $S = 0$, $G_1 \in A$; while if $S = 1$, $G_1 \notin A$. The probability that $X^{(1)}$ can be had without a strike is (from Table 7-2) 0.7. Therefore, $P_{X^{(1)}}(G_1 \in A) = \lambda_1(X^{(1)}) = 0.7$.

Table 7-4

A's Objective	If opposition advocates:								
	$X^{(1)}$			$X^{(2)}$			$X^{(3)}$		
	λ_1	λ_2	λ_3	λ_1	λ_2	λ_3	λ_1	λ_2	λ_3
$X^{(1)}$	—	—	—	0.7	0.0	0.7	1.0	0.0	0.7
$X^{(2)}$	0.2	1.0	0.2	—	—	—	1.0	0.0	1.0
$X^{(3)}$	0.0	1.0	0.0	0.0	1.0	0.5	—	—	—

But what the opposition advocates under a particular circumstance depends on the number of votes it will get. Thus, if the outcome should be $X^{(2)}, S = 1$, Table 7-3A tells us that our opposition would campaign on $X^{(1)}$ and win the election with the votes of G_1 and G_3. Only a dissident faction which was inept or subsidized or which preferred doctrinal purity to holding office would advocate $X^{(3)}$, a position which would yield it only the minority of votes coming from G_2.

From Table 7-3A we can deduce the appropriate opposition response and the electoral consequences of each possible outcome.

Table 7-5

Bargaining Outcome	Opposition Advocates	Election Result
$X^{(1)}, S = 0$	$X^{(2)}$ or $X^{(3)}$	A wins with G_1 and G_3.
$X^{(1)}, S = 1$	$X^{(2)}$	Opp. wins with G_1, G_2, and G_3.
$X^{(2)}, S = 0$	$X^{(3)}$	A wins with G_1 and G_3.
$X^{(2)}, S = 1$	$X^{(1)}$	Opp. wins with G_1 and G_3.
$X^{(3)}, S = 0$	$X^{(1)}$	Opp. wins with G_1 and G_3.
$X^{(3)}, S = 1$	$X^{(1)}$ or $X^{(2)}$	Opp. wins with G_1 and G_3.

Using the affiliation sets implied by the opposition's vote-maximizing behavior, we can now derive

$$R[\lambda(X)] = P\left[\sum_{j=1}^{3} (n_j \mid n_j \in A) > \frac{N}{2}\right].$$

Table 7-6

If A picks	R = probability of winning election
$X^{(1)}$	$= P(S = 0) = 0.7$
$X^{(2)}$	$= P(S = 0) = 0.2$
$X^{(3)}$	$= 0.0$

Hence, $X^{(1)} >_u X^{(2)} >_u X^{(3)}$.

We have already mentioned four limitations of this analysis. First, union elections are contested partly on issues other than the bargaining outcome. Second, to the extent that intraunion communications are imperfect or imperfectly used by the contestants, the opposition may be able to present different programs to different groups without being rejected as liars. Third, at the time of election the majority rank ordering over the alternatives being considered may include a majority set rather than a unique majority alternative. In the context of uncertainty, the alternatives being considered will include the actual outcome of the bargaining as opposed to other possible objectives, with probabilities of different values of S and of any dependent k's taken into account. If there is no unique X_m and the members simply vote their preferences, the leadership is foredoomed because there is always an alternative within the majority set which a majority prefers to the actual outcome. But it may be supposed that the incumbents will win if the outcome is in the majority set; we have argued for the plausibility of voting behavior which leads to this result provided that the groups know each others' preferences.

Fourth, the contestants for office will try to influence by their propaganda both the retrospective probabilities with which the groups view the course of what might have been and their feelings about—and hence choices among—alternatives which include such probabilities. Our theory does not attempt to account for the results of this process or for the many other variables which determine group preferences. This limitation is similar to that of standard microeconomic theory, which takes consumer preferences as given and does not seek to explain just how they are determined.

Our analysis implies that an established opposition may limit substantially the freedom of incumbent officers to pursue such subsidiary goals as the maximization of net revenue, or the minimization of employer or governmental antagonism. As we have seen, the constraint will be most severe if the membership regards the two factions as perfect substitutes in every respect save the bargaining objectives which they achieve or advocate. A rival union, if similarly regarded, could provide the same constraint. The case of perfect substitutability must, of course, be regarded as a limiting rather than as a typical case. But (to reiterate an earlier conclusion) when many members regard rival slates (or rival unions) as fairly close substitutes, a leadership is apt to follow a more "militant" policy than it would otherwise do. And, once again, a union with a strong internal opposition is relatively likely to lose members among any craft or other minorities whose policy preferences differ significantly from those of the majority and whose circumstances make it relatively easy to leave (e.g. where they can transfer allegiance to an established rival union through an electoral process).

While the established opposition is by no means an unknown phenomenon in trade union history, contested elections on the national level have been the exception rather than the rule.[3] But infrequency

---

[3] Philip Taft, *The Structure and Government of Labor Unions* (Cambridge: Harvard University Press, 1954), pp. 35–41.

of contests for office does not always mean that the leadership can afford to ignore the wishes of the rank and file. In the absence of the widespread use of such means of assuring leadership security as outright terrorism or the explusion of dissenters, the lack of an organized opposition *may* indicate that the incumbents have followed policies acceptable enough so that no important segment of the membership has become disaffected enough to take the trouble to form an opposition. Many policies sufficiently distasteful to induce a group to vote for an established opposition may still not be distasteful enough to provoke the same group into organizing an opposition where none exists.

The ease or difficulty with which opposition can arise will depend in part upon the organization's internal structure. Where a substantial proportion of the members can contact each other without incurring large costs, the effort involved in establishing a serious opposition will be reduced. Hence, we would expect the formation of an opposition to be easier in small unions than in large ones, and to be easier when most of the membership is geographically concentrated than when it is widely dispersed. Taft's finding that serious contests for office have been more frequent at the local than at the national level seems consistent with these hypotheses, although it is true that some locals have more members than many internationals.[4] The likelihood that an opposition will arise should be greater when regional officers are elected, and thus have independent political bases, than when they are appointed from the top. It is affected by laws and by judicial decisions. For example, the Labor-Management Reporting and Disclosure ("Landrum-Griffin") Act of 1959 made it more difficult for national unions to impose trusteeships on their local affiliates and created new appeals procedures whereby "outs" can contest vote tallies conducted by the incumbents.

Opposition formation may take the shape of an upsurge of popular sentiment with inexperienced leaders arising from the rank and file, or may occur as a split in a hitherto united leadership with a minority of the union's officers challenging the majority for control. Once an opposition has formed, the leadership, to continue in office, must pick a policy designed to be acceptable to a majority. As we have seen, such a requirement may force the abandonment of secondary objectives: the dictates of the majority may force the leader-

---

[4]Philip Taft, "The Internal Characteristics of American Unions," *Annals of the American Academy of Political Science,* 274 (March 1951), p. 100.

ship to yield occupational or regional minorities to rival unions, or to deplete the treasury in costly strikes when the majority is in a militant mood. If there is no established opposition, particularly in an organization of such size and structure that opposition formation requires considerable effort, the safest policy for the leadership is one sufficiently satisfactory to so many of the groups that no significant bloc will undertake the effort of founding an opposition (and, incidentally, no dissenter among the incumbent officers will see advantage in helping to do so). To some groups, perhaps enough to constitute a majority of the membership, the policy which the union adopts under these circumstances may be less desirable than that which would have been chosen had an established opposition been present. Other groups, however, may be better off.

We shall now deduce the preference ordering of the leadership when the problem is not to defeat an existing opposition but to prevent one from coming into being. Formally, the analysis of a leadership trying to prevent the formation of an opposition is similar to that of the union trying to win an organizational strike.

Let $\mathring{G}$ be the set of all possible subsets of G. And let V' be a subset of $\mathring{G}$ such that it contains all those elements (subsets of G) and only those elements in $\mathring{G}$ such that the support of such a subset for the leadership will prevent the formation of an opposition.

We shall also substitute $\overset{*}{\in}$ for $\in$. $G_j' \overset{*}{\in} A$ means that G_j' would *not* participate in forming an opposition if the possibility of doing so arose.

Let $R'(X) = P[(\text{all } G_j \mid G_j \overset{*}{\in} A) \in V']$. For example, $R'(X^{(1)})$ is the probability—given the $P_i(K^i)$ and $P(S(X^{(1)}))$ distributions—that, if $X^{(1)}$ is adopted as the union's bargaining objective and then achieved, the subset of groups which *refrains* from participating in the formation of an opposition will be a subset such that the remaining, "dissident" groups will fail to establish an alternative party. (After developing the formal union preference ordering implied in such a case, we shall try to explain below why such a model might account for some organizational behavior.)

If we presume as in the previous leadership case that these internal considerations will affect union preferences only among objectives yielding "satisfactory" and/or equal probabilities of union survival, the union preference ordering will now be:

(1) $(\rho(X^{(2)}) < \mathring{\rho}) \rightarrow \{[\rho(X^{(1)}) > \rho(X^{(2)})] \rightarrow [X^{(1)} >_u X^{(2)}]\}.$

(2) $\{\rho(X^{(1)}) \geq \mathring{\rho} \text{ and } \rho(X^{(2)}) \geq \mathring{\rho}\} \rightarrow$
$$\{[R'(X^{(1)}) > R'(X^{(2)})] \leftrightarrow [X^{(1)} >_u X^{(2)}]\}.$$

(3) $\{\rho(X^{(1)}) < \overset{\circ}{\rho}$ and $\rho(X^{(2)}) < \overset{\circ}{\rho}$ and $\rho(X^{(1)}) = \rho(X^{(2)})\} \rightarrow$
$$\{[R'(X^{(1)}) > R'(X^{(2)})] \leftrightarrow [X^{(1)} >_u X^{(2)}]\}.$$

(4) $\{\rho(X^{(1)}) < \overset{\circ}{\rho}$ and $\rho(X^{(2)}) < \overset{\circ}{\rho}$ and $\rho(X^{(1)}) = \rho(X^{(2)})\} \rightarrow$
$$\{[R'(X^{(1)}) = R'(X^{(2)})] \leftrightarrow [X^{(1)} \sim_u X^{(2)}]\}.$$

(5) $\{\rho(X^{(1)}) > \overset{\circ}{\rho}$ and $\rho(X^{(2)}) > \overset{\circ}{\rho}\} \rightarrow$
$$\{[R'(X^{(1)}) = R'(X^{(2)})] \leftrightarrow [X^{(1)} \sim_u X^{(2)}]\}.$$

Except for the replacement of R with R', this is identical with the preceding case.

The above is intended as a model of a one-party union, in contrast with a two-party union. In the latter, very little effort is required by a group if it wishes to express disaffection with the incumbents by voting to oust them. In the former, setting up an opposition slate certainly requires some effort, and very often a great deal of it. (Organizing an opposition in many one-party organizations may also involve the risk of penalties for the organizers.)

Bearing this in mind, let us suppose that, as a mental experiment, we leave unchanged everything about a union except that we vary its structure from a two-party to a one-party organization. We will expect that for some groups there will be situations $(X, S(X), K)$ leading to disaffiliation under the two-party arrangement $(G_j \nsubseteq A)$, which same situations would imply affiliation under the one-party regime $(G_j \overset{*}{\in} A)$. We would not expect the opposite case. The one-party regime, then, has more "leeway." It is apt, *ceteris paribus,* to have a larger batch of objectives yielding (R')'s above some value than is the leadership in a two-party organization. If it is "on its toes," it may be better able than its two-party counterpart to come up with solutions which are "satisfactory" in terms of both its own needs and those of the organization in the face of group preference orderings which diverge rather considerably from each other.

But it must act within limits if it is to retain its unchallenged control, somewhat as a monopolist may have to stop short of profit maximization if he is to forestall entry.

One possible model of a one-party union would be identical to that developed for the two-party case; this would be followed by a paragraph to the effect that, because of the effort involved in forming an opposition where none is established, the λ's for many groups and many X's—and hence, the R's for many X's—in such an organization will be larger, *ceteris paribus,* than in a two-party union. In this version, the leadership would prefer that bargaining objective which maximized its chances of reelection if it should be challenged.

The "subset" model above is meant to suggest something else. The leadership in a one-party organization has an interest in preventing an opposition from forming. (In real life, we might qualify this and speak of a "serious" opposition.) The mere establishment of an opposition would reduce the number of alternatives which the leadership had available to it. The resulting leadership preference ordering need not be identical to that of a leadership faced with an extant opposition. (That is, $R(X^{(1)}) > R(X^{(2)})$ does not always imply $R'(X^{(1)}) > R'(X^{(2)})$.) We shall now try to suggest to what sort of real world subset the R' model might apply.

V' was defined as a subset of $\mathring{G}$ containing all those subsets of $\mathcal{G}$ such that the support of such a subset would prevent the formation of an opposition. In the model which followed, the leadership, given satisfactory ρ's, sought to maximize the probability that it would get such support that no opposition would be formed.

If $\mathcal{G}$, then, were to consist of $\{G_1, G_2, G_3, G_4, G_5\}$; and if lack of the affiliation of any two of these groups would suffice to form an opposition, then V' would consist of:

$$G_1, G_2, G_3, G_4, G_5.$$
$$G_1, G_2, G_3, G_4.$$
$$G_1, G_2, G_3, G_5.$$
$$G_1, G_3, G_4, G_5.$$
$$G_2, G_3, G_4, G_5.$$

Its complement, $\overline{V}'$, is defined to include all other subsets of $\mathring{G}$. If all $G_j \mid G_j \overset{*}{\in} A$ were in $\overline{V}'$, an opposition would be formed.

We shall mention two kinds of situations in which such a model might apply; by no means do we claim the list to be exhaustive.

The first is a rather mechanical one. Suppose that a rule in the union's constitution provides that candidates for international offices may be nominated by the incumbent executive board (which we shall assume to present a united front) or by petitions signed by at least 30% of the members with one or more signatures coming from at least 50% of the locals. Here, $R'(X^{(1)})$ is the probability that if $X^{(1)}$ is the bargaining outcome, then the groups *not* willing to sign petitions for anti-incumbent candidates will be of such size and geographical dispersion that the remaining members (who are willing to sign) will either number less than 30% of the membership or will be concentrated in fewer than 50% of the locals, or both. In the absence of an explicit rule of this sort, a leadership might act as if some such rule were there, for a group disaffected enough to be willing to form an opposition is more likely to take action if it knows that other groups are similarly inclined.

As a second situation, suppose that no opposition (or at least no "serious" opposition) can in fact be mounted unless at least one member of the International Executive Board aligns himself with it. Suppose further that no such board member will do such a thing unless two or more groups constituting 25% or more of the membership go along with him. We are not thinking here of possible constitutional provisions to this effect, but of the facts that international officers travel to various locals, that some groups willing to support a slate headed by an experienced officer might reject a strictly rank and file slate for fear it might botch up its job regardless of intentions, and that many of the recorded contests for international union office have in fact involved splits in the executive.[5] In this case, V' includes all subsets of G which include all members of the Board; and any subset of G accounting for at least 75% of the membership will meet this requirement.

As we saw in Chapter IV, dissatisfied occupational and regional minorities sometimes engage in another form of "disaffiliation" by attaching themselves to (or, sometimes, establishing) rival unions. Where the minority is occupational, this is often a union specializing in the problems of a particular group of crafts, and the N.L.R.B.'s "Globe election" policies have made such alternatives readily available as well as attractive to some occupational groups. We concluded that a one-party union would often find it easier to retain the support of all electoral units than would a two-party union.

Once again, we shall adjust our model to allow for the possibility of more than one election unit. To do this, some alterations in our formal structure are required. The original Definition i, repeated below, is restored.

Definition i.
  $G = \{G_1, G_2, \ldots G_j, \ldots G_m\}$. $G_1 \cup G_2 \cup \ldots G_j \cup \ldots \cup G_m = E$, and for all G'_j, G''_j, $G'_j \cap G''_j = \Lambda$.

Definition *xi*, below, is added to provide for a set of election districts.

Definition xi.
  $\mathfrak{D} = \{D_1, D_2, \ldots D_f, \ldots D_w\}$. $D_1 \cup D_2 \cup \ldots \cup D_f \cup \ldots \cup D_w = E$, and for all D'_f, D''_f, $D'_f \cap D''_f = \Lambda$.

---

[5] Several examples are mentioned in Taft, *The Structure and Government of Labor Unions*, Ch. 2.

Since we must talk both of numbers in a group and of numbers in an election district, let ng_j be the number of individuals in the jth group and nd_f the number of individuals in the fth election district. Also, let $nd_f g_j$ be the number of individuals from the jth group who are in the fth election district. We now stipulate that the number of individuals in the groups and the number of individuals in the districts are the same.

Axiom vii.

$$\sum_{j=1}^{m} ng_j = \sum_{f=1}^{w} nd_f = N$$

This arrangement relieves us of any necessity of making election districts correspond precisely to groups, while allowing groups to be concentrated in particular election districts. For example, D_1 might consist of all ten employees classed as skilled electricians in a plant; G_1 of nine of these electricians sharing identical preferences over (X, K, S) and especially about electricians' rates; and G_2 of twenty black workers, including the tenth electrician, with unique preferences of their own, especially about negro upgrading.

With separate elections in each district, we can speak of a ρ for each D.

Definition xii.

$$\rho_f = P\left[\sum_{j=1}^{m} \left(\frac{nd_f g_j}{nd_f} \,\middle|\, nd_f g_j \in T \right) > 0.5 \right].$$

Several union preference orderings, and indeed whole families of preference orderings suggest themselves as possible in the multi-district case, and the greater the number of districts the more such orderings there are. Even in a two-district situation, a union might be thought of as seeking to win both districts (maximize $\rho_1 \rho_2$), or to win at least one (maximize $\rho_1 + \rho_2 - \rho_1 \rho_2$), or aim at winning both so long as the chances of success in at least one were satisfactory, or act in terms of some indifference map of the two suggested maximands. We shall not attempt to argue for one or another of these possible criteria. Instead, we shall limit ourselves to the case where there are two election districts, one of which is secure in the sense that $\rho(X)$ is large for many X, while the other is not at all secure. A rival union may be seeking to organize it, or it may be inclined to give up union representation. Our aim is to show formally that the leadership of a one-party union may find it easier to retain the affiliation of such a group than would the leadership of a two-party union.

Suppose now that $\mathring{R}(X)$ and $\mathring{R}'(X)$ designate "satisfactory" values of R and R'. That is, in choosing among bargaining objectives with $R > \mathring{R}$ (or $R' > \mathring{R}'$), a leadership will feel free to base its preferences on criteria other than the retention of office or the prevention of the rise of an opposition.

Let the secure election district be called D_1 and the insecure one D_2. If the leadership seeks to retain D_2's affiliation to the union provided that the probability of its own retention in office is satisfactory, then

$$R > \mathring{R} \leftrightarrow [(\rho_2(X^{(1)}) > \rho_2(X^{(2)}) \rightarrow X^{(1)} >_u X^{(2)}].$$

And if the leadership is similarly inclined, provided that the probability that an opposition will not be formed is satisfactory, then:

$$R' > \mathring{R}' \rightarrow [(\rho_2(X^{(1)}) > \rho_2(X^{(2)}) \rightarrow X^{(1)} >_u X^{(2)}].$$

As we have seen, the difficulties of establishing an opposition in a one-party union are likely to result in a situation in which some values of (X, K, S) imply both $G_j \notin A$ and $G_j \stackrel{*}{\in} A$. We have no basis for supposing the opposite case. There may, then, be bargaining objectives yielding relatively high values of ρ_2 which at the same time imply "unsafe" values of R—$R(X) < \mathring{R}$—but "safe" values of $R'(R'(X) > \mathring{R}')$. The inclusion of uncertainty in our model, then, does nothing to detract from our earlier conclusion that the leadership of a one-party union may be relatively successful at preserving against external threats an organization composed of a somewhat heterogeneous rank and file.

Our family of formal theories of union behavior is now complete. One final cautionary observation is in order. Much of the concern of this book, particularly in the last few chapters, is with the internal aspects of that behavior. This may leave the reader with a misconception of the relative importance we attach to "political" as opposed to "economic" determinants of bargaining objectives. The apparent emphasis on the former follows unavoidably from the necessity to devote so much of the exposition to the more novel features of the present approach. While changes in internal political structures or in external rules governing the award of representational rights may be quite important (as in 1935–1940 in the United States), we do not imply that such matters play a greater part in union decisions than do economic events which affect the demand for labor, employers' willingness to withstand strikes, and employees' levels of economic well-being. The primacy of economic events as determinants is of course unchallenged. But the ways in which these events affect a union's policies may be significantly and systematically molded, so to speak, by the shapes of the political channels through which they are transmitted. A main objective of this treatise is to demonstrate that *both* "political" and "economic" aspects of an organization's behavior can be treated within the same theoretical framework.

APPENDIX TO CHAPTERS V, VI, AND VII

List of Definitions and Axioms

I. The following definitions and axioms are used in developing our model of a survival-oriented union faced with the threat of loss of its bargaining rights in an N.L.R.B.-type election, as this model is set forth in Chapters V and VI.

Definition i. Groups.
$\mathcal{G} = \{G_1, G_2, \ldots G_j, \ldots G_m\}$. $G_1 \cup G_2 \cup \ldots \cup G_j \cup \ldots \cup G_m = E$, and for all $G_{j'}, G_{j''}, G_{j'} \cap G_{j''} = \Lambda$, the empty set.

Definition ii. The Bargainable Variables.
$\mathcal{X} = \{x_1 \times x_2 \times \ldots \times x_i \times \ldots \times x_n\}$ = the set of all $(x_1^i, \ldots x_i^i, \ldots x_n^i)$ such that $x_1^i \in x_1$, and $\ldots$ and $x_i^i \in x_i$ and $\ldots$ and $x_n^i \in x_n$. Thought of as a set of vectors, $\mathcal{X} = \{X \mid X = (x_1, x_2, \ldots x_i, \ldots x_n)\}$.

Definition iii. The Nonbargainable Variables.
$\mathcal{K} = \{k_1 \times k_2 \times \ldots \times k_i \times \ldots \times k_r\}$ = the set of all $(k_1^i, \ldots k_i^i, \ldots k_r^i)$ such that $k_1^i \in k_1$ and $\ldots$ and $k_i^i \in k_i$ and $\ldots$ and $k_r^i \in k_r$. $\mathcal{K} = \{K \mid K = (k_1, k_2, \ldots k_i, \ldots k_r)\}$.

Axiom i. The Strike Length Function.
$$S = f(X); \; S \geq 0.$$

Definition iv. The Set of Attainable Bargaining Outcomes.
$$\overset{*}{\mathcal{X}} = \{X \mid X \in \mathcal{X} \text{ and } S = f(X)\}.$$

Axiom i (a). The Modified Strike Length Function.
$$S = f(X, K); \; S \geq 0.$$

Definition iv (a). The Set of Attainable Outcomes.
$$\overset{*}{\mathcal{X}}(K^i) = \{X \mid X \in \mathcal{X} \text{ and } (K = K^i) \to S = f(X)\}.$$

Axiom ii. Every Group Is Affiliated or Not Affiliated with the Union.
For all G_j, either $G_j \in T$ or $G_j \notin T$.

Axiom iii. Group Affiliation and Group Preferences.
For all G_j, $\{(X, K)^{(1)} \to (G_j \in T) \text{ and } (X, K)^{(2)} \to (G_j \notin T)\} \to (X, K)^{(1)} >_j (X, K)^{(2)}\}$.

Axiom iv. Group Affiliation and Group Preferences (More).

For all G_j, $\{(X, K)^{(1)} \rightarrow (G_j \in T)$ and $(X, K)^{(1)} \sim (X, K)^{(2)}\} \rightarrow \{(X, K)^{(2)} \rightarrow (G_j \in T)\}$.

Axiom v. An Unattainable Outcome Implies Non-Affiliation.

For all $G_j, X \notin \overset{*}{\mathfrak{X}} \rightarrow G_j \notin T$.

Definition v. The Number of Affiliated Individuals.

Let n_j be the number of individuals in G_j and let $N = \sum_{j=1}^{m} n_j$, which is the number of individuals for whom the union has or seeks representational rights. $G_{j'} \in T \rightarrow n_{j'} \in T$. To every $(X, K)^i$ there corresponds some $\sum_{j=1}^{m} n_j \mid n_j \in T$.

Definition vi. The Cartesian product, $\mathcal{W}$.

$\mathcal{W} = \mathcal{K} \cdot \mathcal{S}$, where $\mathcal{K} = \{K^{(1)}, K^{(2)}, \ldots\}$ and $\mathcal{S} = \{S^{(1)}, S^{(2)}, \ldots\}$.

Each element in this set consists of one of the possible values of K and one of the possible values of S.

Definition vii. Partition of $\mathcal{W}$.

$$\overset{*}{\mathcal{W}}(X^i, G_{j'}) = \{W \mid W \in \overset{*}{\mathcal{W}}(X^i, G_{j'}) \leftrightarrow G_{j'} \in T\}.$$

Definition viii. Probability of a Group's Affiliation in the Event of Each Possible Bargaining Outcome.

$$\text{Let } \pi_{j'}(X) = P(W(X) \in \overset{*}{\mathcal{W}}_{j'}) = P_X(G_{j'} \in T).$$

Definition ix. The Set of Vectors of Such Affiliation Probabilities.

$$\Pi = \{\pi \mid \pi = \pi_1(X), \pi_2(X), \ldots \pi_j(X), \ldots \pi_m(X)\}$$

Definition x. The Probability of Winning an N.L.R.B.-Type Election.

$$\text{Let } \rho(\pi(X)) = P\left[\sum_{j=1}^{m} (n_j \mid n_j \in T) > \frac{N}{2}\right].$$

Axiom vi. The "Satisfactory" Probability of Union Survival.

Let $\overset{\circ}{\rho}$ be some value of $\rho(X)$.

The union's preference ordering over alternative bargaining outcomes in this case is:

$$\rho(X^{(1)}) < \overset{\circ}{\rho}$$

or

$$\rho(X^{(2)}) < \overset{\circ}{\rho} \leftrightarrow \{[\rho(X^{(1)}) > \rho(X^{(2)})] \leftrightarrow (X^{(1)} >_u X^{(2)})\}$$

and

$$\{[\rho(X^{(1)}) = \rho(X^{(2)})] \leftrightarrow (X^{(1)} \sim_u X^{(2)})\}.$$

Among outcomes with $\rho(X^i) > \overset{\circ}{\rho}$, the union's preferences will be based on some supplementary criterion.

II. Toward the close of Chapter VI, a second model is developed in which the union is faced with the threat of loss of its bargaining rights as a consequence of an unsuccessful organizational strike. We retain definitions *i* through *ix* and Axioms *i* through *v*. But the last definition (*x*) and the last axiom (*vi*) are modified as follows:

Definition x (b). The Probability of Winning an Organizational Strike.
Let $\overset{\circ}{G}$ be the set of all possible subsets of $\mathcal{G}$.
Let V be a subset of $\overset{\circ}{G}$. V should be interpreted as referring to the subset of $\overset{\circ}{G}$ which contains all those subsets of $\mathcal{G}$, the affiliation of which with the union implies its survival.
Let $\rho'[\pi(X)] = P[(\text{all } G'_j \mid G'_j \in T) \in V]$.
Axiom vi (b). The "Satisfactory" Probability of Union Survival.
Let $\overset{\circ}{\rho}'$ be some value of $\rho'(X)$.
The union's preference ordering over alternative bargaining outcomes in this case is:
$$\rho'(X^{(1)}) < \overset{\circ}{\rho}'$$

or

$$\rho'(X^{(2)}) < \overset{\circ}{\rho}' \leftrightarrow X^{(1)} >_u X^{(2)} \leftrightarrow \rho'[\pi(X^{(1)})] > \rho'[\pi(X^{(2)})]$$

and

$$X^{(1)} \sim_u X^{(2)} \leftrightarrow \rho'[\pi(X^{(1)})] = \rho'[\pi(X^{(2)})].$$

III. In Chapter VII, we turn to a union faced with the threat of ouster from office by an established internal opposition. Our set of definitions and axioms is modified as follows:

Definition i (c). Groups.
$\mathcal{G} = \{G_1, G_2, \dots G_j, \dots G_m\}$. $G_1 \cup G_2 \cup \dots \cup G_j \cup \dots \cup G_m = T$, and for all $G_{j'}, G_{j''}, G_{j'} \cap G_{j''} = \Lambda$, the empty set.

Definitions ii, iii, and iv remain the same.

Definition v (c). The Number of Affiliated Individuals.
Let n_j be the number of individuals in G_j and let $N = \sum_{j=1}^{m} n_j$, which is the number of individuals eligible to vote for the retention or ouster of the leadership. $G_{j'} \in A \rightarrow n_{j'} \in A$. To every $(X, K)^1$ there corresponds some $\sum_{j=1}^{m} n_j \mid n_j \in A$.

Definition vi remains the same.

Definition vii (c). Partition of $\mathcal{W}$.

$$\overline{\mathcal{W}}(X^i, G_j') = \{W \mid W \in \overline{\mathcal{W}}(X^i, G_j') \hookleftarrow (G_j' \in A)\}.$$

Definition viii (c). Probability of a Group's Affiliation in the Event of Each Possible Bargaining Outcome.

$$\text{Let } \lambda_j'(X) = P(W(X) \in \overline{\mathcal{W}}_i') = P_X(G_i' \in A).$$

Definition ix (c). The Set of Vectors of Such Affiliation Probabilities.

$$L = \{\lambda \mid \lambda = \lambda_1(X), \lambda_2(X), \ldots \lambda_j(X), \ldots \lambda_m(X)\}.$$

Definition x (c). The Probability of Retention in Office for a Leadership Faced with an Established Opposition.

$$\text{Let } R(\lambda(X)) = P\left[\sum_{j=1}^{m} (n_j \mid n_j \in A) > \frac{N}{2}\right].$$

Axiom i stands as before.
Axiom ii (*c*). Every Group Is Affiliated or Not Affiliated with the Administration.

For all G_j, either $G_j \in A$ or $G_j \notin A$.
Axioms iii and *iv* are dropped.
Axiom v (*c*). An Unattainable Outcome Implies Non-Affiliation.

For all $G_j, X \notin \overset{*}{\mathcal{X}} \to G_j \notin A$.

Axiom vi remains the same.

Presuming that survival of the union takes precedence over retention of the leadership in office, the union's preference ordering will be, in this case:

$$(\rho(X^{(2)}) < \overset{\circ}{\rho}) \to \{[\rho(X^{(1)}) > \rho(X^{(2)})] \to [X^{(1)} >_u X^{(2)}]\}.$$
$$\{\rho(X^{(1)}) \geq \overset{\circ}{\rho}$$

and

$$\rho(X^{(2)}) \geq \overset{\circ}{\rho}\} \to \{[R(X^{(1)}) > R(X^{(2)})] \hookleftarrow [X^{(1)} >_u X^{(2)}]\}.$$
$$\{\rho(X^{(1)}) < \overset{\circ}{\rho}$$

and

$$\rho(X^{(2)}) < \overset{\circ}{\rho}$$

and

$$\rho(X^{(1)}) = \rho(X^{(2)})\} \leftrightarrow \{[R(X^{(1)}) > R(X^{(2)})] \leftrightarrow$$
$$[X^{(1)} >_u X^{(2)}]\}.$$

IV. Toward the close of Chapter VII, we consider a leadership seeking to prevent the formation of an opposition. Most of the Definitions and Axioms used in the third case are used here, too. However, the symbol $\in$ must be replaced, wherever it appears, by $\overset{*}{\in}$. We also have a new version of Definition x.

Definition x (d). The Probability of Preventing Formation of an Opposition.

Let $\overset{\circ}{G}$ be the set of all possible subsets of $\mathcal{G}$. And let V' be a subset of $\overset{\circ}{G}$ such that it contains all those elements (subsets of $\mathcal{G}$) and only those elements in $\overset{\circ}{G}$ such that the support of such a subset for the leadership will prevent the formation of an opposition.

$$\text{Let } R'(X) = P[(\text{all } G_j \mid G_j \overset{*}{\in} A) \in V'].$$

In this case, the union's preference ordering will be:

(1) $(\rho(X^{(2)}) < \overset{\circ}{\rho}) \rightarrow \{[\rho(X^{(1)}) > \rho(X^{(2)})] \rightarrow [X^{(1)} >_u X^{(2)}]\}.$

(2) $\{\rho(X^{(1)}) \geq \overset{\circ}{\rho} \text{ and } (X^{(2)}) \geq \overset{\circ}{\rho}\} \rightarrow$
$$\{[R'(X^{(1)}) > R'(X^{(2)})] \leftrightarrow [X^{(1)} >_u X^{(2)}]\}.$$

(3) $\{\rho(X^{(1)}) < \overset{\circ}{\rho} \text{ and } \rho(X^{(2)}) < \overset{\circ}{\rho} \text{ and } \rho(X^{(1)}) = \rho(X^{(2)})\} \rightarrow$
$$\{[R'(X^{(1)}) > R'(X^{(2)})] \leftrightarrow [X^{(1)} >_u X^{(2)}]\}.$$

(4) $\{\rho(X^{(1)}) < \overset{\circ}{\rho} \text{ and } \rho(X^{(2)}) < \overset{\circ}{\rho} \text{ and } \rho(X^{(1)}) = \rho(X^{(2)})\} \rightarrow$
$$\{[R'(X^{(1)}) = R'(X^{(2)})] \leftrightarrow [X^{(1)} \sim_u X^{(2)}]\}.$$

(5) $\{\rho(X^{(1)}) > \overset{\circ}{\rho} \text{ and } \rho(X^{(2)}) > \overset{\circ}{\rho}\} \rightarrow$
$$\{[R'(X^{(1)}) = R'(X^{(2)})] \leftrightarrow [X^{(1)} \sim_u X^{(2)}]\}.$$

V. Finally, in adjusting our model to allow for the possibility of more than one election unit, two more definitions and another axiom are added.

Definition xi. The Set of Election Districts.

$\mathfrak{D} = \{D_1, D_2, \ldots D_f, \ldots D_w\}. D_1 \cup D_2 \cup \ldots \cup D_f \cup \ldots \cup D_w = E$, and for all $D'_f, D''_f, D'_f \cap D''_f = \Lambda$.

Axiom vii. Every Member of a Group Belongs to One Election District.

Letting ng_j be the number of individuals in the j'th group and nd_f the number of individuals in the f'th election district,

$$\sum_{j=1}^{m} ng_j = \sum_{f=1}^{w} nd_f = N$$

Letting $nd_f g_j$ be the number of individuals from the j'th group who are in the f'th election, we can define a ρ for each D.

Definition xii. Probability of Winning the f'th Election District.

$$\rho_f = P\left[\sum_{j=1}^{m} \left(\frac{nd_f g_j}{nd_f} \mid nd_f g_j \in T\right) > 0.5\right].$$

INDEX